Fortifications

Special Forces Camps in Vietnam 1961–70

Gordon L Rottman · Illustrated by Chris Taylor

Series editors Marcus Cowper and Nikolai Bogdanovic

First published in 2005 by Osprey Publishing, Midland House,
West Way, Botley, Oxford OX2 0PH, UK
443 Park Avenue South, New York, NY 10016, USA
E-mail: info@ospreypublishing.com

ISBN 1 84603 070 6

Design: Ken Vail Graphic Design, Cambridge, UK
Index by Bob Munro
Originated by The Electronic Page Company, Cwmbran, UK
Printed in China through Bookbuilders

05 06 07 08 09   10 9 8 7 6 5 4 3 2 1

A CIP catalog record for this book is available from the British Library.

FOR A CATALOG OF ALL BOOKS PUBLISHED BY OSPREY MILITARY AND AVIATION
PLEASE CONTACT:

NORTH AMERICA
Osprey Direct, 2427 Bond Street, University Park, IL 60466, USA
E-mail: info@ospreydirectusa.com

ALL OTHER REGIONS
Osprey Direct UK, P.O. Box 140, Wellingborough, Northants, NN8 2FA, UK
E-mail: info@ospreydirect.co.uk

www.ospreypublishing.com

Author's acknowledgments

The author is indebted to Colonel Roger H. C. Donlon, former
commander of Detachment A-726, for his insight on the layout
of Camp Nam Dong and the July 1964 attack. The author is also
very grateful to Steve Sherman of RADIX Press for the research
materials, photographs, and advice he provided. Frank M. Thomas,
a former combat artist, was kind enough to provide two of his
prints to illustrate this book.

Image credits

Unless otherwise indicated, the photographic images and line
drawings that appear in this work are from the author's collection
and US Government sources.

Measurements

Distances, ranges, and dimensions of materials and
constructions are given in inches, feet, yards, and statute miles
rather than metric:

inches to centimeters	multiply inches by 2.540
feet to meters	multiply feet by 0.3048
yards to meters	multiply yards by 0.9144
miles to kilometers	multiply miles by 1.6093

Artist's note

Readers may care to note that prints of *Nam Dong Standoff* (p.47)
and *CIDG Hunter-Killers* (p. 5) are available for private sale. All
enquires should be addressed to:

Frank M. Thomas
Wild Goose Creek Studios
210 North 100 East
Holden, Utah 85636
USA
http://www.wildgoosecreekstudio.com/

The Publishers regret that they can enter into no correspondence
upon this matter.

The Fortress Study Group (FSG)

The object of the FSG is to advance the education of the public
in the study of all aspects of fortifications and their armaments,
especially works constructed to mount or resist artillery. The FSG
holds an annual conference in September over a long weekend
with visits and evening lectures, an annual tour abroad lasting
about eight days, and an annual Members' Day.
   The FSG journal *FORT* is published annually, and its newsletter
Casemate is published three times a year. Membership is interna-
tional. For further details, please contact:
The Secretary, c/o 6 Lanark Place, London W9 1BS, UK

Contents

Introduction

US Army Special Forces (USSF) was organized in 1952 and trained to infiltrate behind enemy lines during a conventional or nuclear war, make contact with indigenous resistance forces, develop a rapport with the partisans, and organize, train and supply them to conduct a guerrilla war in the enemy's rear areas. It was originally envisaged to establish partisan forces in Eastern Europe in the event of a Soviet invasion of the West. USSF soon expanded, with new responsibilities assigned for Asia and Latin America. USSF also had other missions. Its personnel were able to train special operations forces of friendly countries along their own lines, recover personnel from behind enemy lines, and collect strategic intelligence information during missions deep within enemy territory.

In 1961, in a country that few had heard of, USSF was tasked with a different mission; one that was essentially the opposite of its primary mission. The Republic of Vietnam (South Vietnam) was immersed in a wide-ranging guerrilla war that was supported by the communist Democratic Republic of Vietnam (North Vietnam). USSF elements were first sent there in 1959 to assist in training South Vietnamese Special Forces. The war continued to escalate and by 1961 it had spread into remote areas, over which the government had little control. Although South Vietnam was a comparatively small country, the extremely rugged land included vast remote areas in the northern mountains, the rolling and forested Central Highlands, the dense jungles in the south-central area, and the endless marshes of the Mekong Delta in the south. There were few roads, many areas being accessible only by air. These remote areas were inhabited by a variety of ethnic minority groups that the Vietnamese usually ignored. The Viet Cong, however, did not ignore them. They not only exploited these primitive peoples, but also converted them to their cause as a result of the South Vietnamese Government's indifference or mistreatment.

It soon became apparent that the Viet Cong (VC) were establishing major base areas in these remote regions and enlisting the support of the local minorities. The locals had little choice in the matter and any resistance on their part was dealt with brutally. If help had been provided, they would rather have sided with the indifferent government of South Vietnam. Communism was not to their liking.

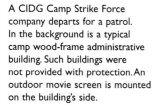

A CIDG Camp Strike Force company departs for a patrol. In the background is a typical camp wood-frame administrative building. Such buildings were not provided with protection. An outdoor movie screen is mounted on the building's side.

USSF was assigned the mission of establishing themselves in these areas, training local security forces to protect villages from the VC, and eventually forming counter-guerrilla forces to harass and destroy the VC. In order to conduct this mission, USSF had to have bases from which to operate. To this end, the first crude camps were established in the Central Highlands in 1961. They were simple, austere, unsophisticated in design, and built from locally available materials. The local forces were recruited under a number of different CIA-sponsored programs (Border Surveillance, Trail Watchers, Mountain Commandos), but in 1962 they were consolidated into the Civilian Irregular Defense Group (CIDG). The CIDG were not part of the Army of the Republic of Vietnam (ARVN), but were essentially mercenaries organized, trained, clothed, fed, equipped, and paid by the US Government.

CIDG Hunter Killers. USSF advisors and CIDG round up Viet Cong suspects in a Montagnard village in northern South Vietnam. Thatch and rattan-built Montagnard long houses (as pictured here) were constructed in the early camps for use as team houses, supply rooms, and barracks. (Frank M. Thomas ®)

Over the years the program grew and the camps evolved. By 1970 there were over 80 camps, each home to a battalion-size strike force tasked with conducting aggressive counter-guerrilla operations throughout South Vietnam. A 12–14-man Special Forces A-team advised each camp alongside a South Vietnamese Special Forces counterpart team.

The camps were located in some of the most remote areas of South Vietnam and on widely varied terrain. Cut off from civilization, they were more akin to Old West frontier army posts within Indian Territory and surrounded by hostile and capable foes. Many were beyond friendly artillery range and very much on their own. As the capabilities of the VC increased, the war escalated, North Vietnamese Army (NVA) regulars moved south, and the camps evolved too.

Camp defenses were improved and hardened to resist large-scale and increasingly aggressive attacks. In 1966 "fighting camps" were developed. All new camps were built under this concept and existing camps were upgraded. If they were too small or had deteriorated from use over a long period of time, they were relocated and new camps built. The fighting camps had increased defenses and an inner perimeter capable of holding out even if the outer perimeter had been penetrated. In the flood-prone Mekong Delta "floating camps" were constructed. Team houses, barracks, supply rooms, ammunition bunkers, and other support facilities were built on floating platforms designed to rise with the floodwaters. Another type was the "subsurface camp," built in some areas adjacent to the border camps that received heavy and frequent shelling. In these locations it made sense that all facilities and quarters were completely buried.

No two camps were alike. They were built to conform to the terrain and the ideas of the USSF team. They may have been square, rectangular, triangular, five-pointed stars, five-, six- or eight-sided, or irregularly shaped. The defenses included mortar and artillery positions, recoilless rifle positions (when the North Vietnamese began using tanks), and machine gun bunkers and towers. Extremely dense and elaborate barbed wire barrier systems surrounded the camps, as did scores of Claymore mines, trip flares, *punji* stakes, and moats in some cases.

The camps were self-contained. Besides housing the strike force, their families often lived in the camps. Power generators provided electricity. There were water wells and reserve rations were sufficient for a 30-day siege. Each camp had a fully equipped dispensary for both the troops and their dependents, a school for the children, barber and tailor shops, a motor pool and vehicle maintenance shop, even a café. Many camps possessed an airstrip and helicopter pad; others in the mountains did not and had to be resupplied by parachute drop.

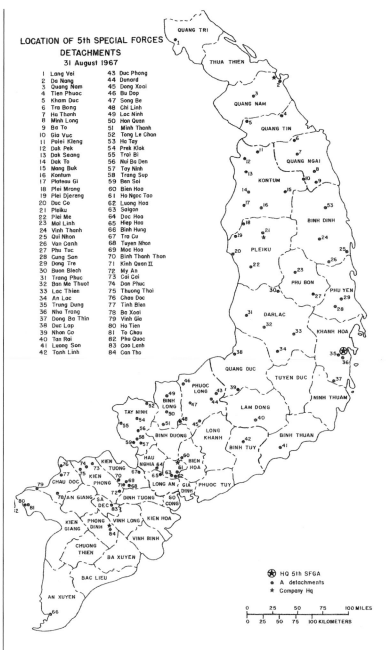

Location of 5th Special Forces
Group detachments, August 1, 1967.

The first camp was built at Buon Enao, a Montagnard tribal village in the remote Central Highlands. In 1961 the VC were exploiting the surrounding region of some 200 villages. Working from this little village with a population of 200, USSF established an expanding system of camps and trained local self-defense forces. By 1962, when the CIDG Program was launched, all 200 villages were protected from the VC. This simple program involved only a few dozen USSF soldiers, but it made higher commands realize that large areas could be secured and brought under government control by employing well-led local forces. This allowed conventional combat forces to conduct offensive operations to search out and destroy the elusive VC. They need not be tied down protecting populations in remote areas from exploitation.

Initially USSF teams were deployed to Vietnam and attached to US Military Advisory Group, Vietnam. In 1962 US Army Special Forces, Vietnam (Provisional) was formed to control all in-country USSF elements. The 1st, 5th, and 7th Special Forces Groups (Airborne) (SFGA) provided the teams on six-month temporary duty tours. In 1964 this provisional structure was replaced by phasing-in the 5th SFGA, which was directly subordinate to US Military Assistance Command, Vietnam (MACV); USSF personnel were rotated for one-year tours. Vietnam was divided into four corps tactical zones (CTZ), with a USSF company being responsible for teams in each CTZ. A USSF "company" is really a misnomer. It consisted of a Special Forces operational detachment C (C-team) commanded by a lieutenant colonel with over 70 USSF personnel, a complete command staff, communications, and logistical support activities with indigenous personnel providing the manpower. It controlled several B-teams (some 30 USSF personnel) located in provincial capitals, which in turn controlled several 12–14-man A-teams responsible for the strike force camps. Each team at all echelons had a counterpart Vietnamese Special Forces team, the *Luc-luong Dac-Biét* (LLDB).

Special Forces' involvement in Vietnam was a complex and multi-facetted affair. This book discusses the strike camps, which played a key role. For further information on Special Forces in Vietnam the reader is referred to the following Osprey books: Elite 4 *US Army Special Forces 1952–84*; Elite 29 *Vietnam Airborne*; and Warrior 28 *Green Beret in Vietnam 1957–73*.

The threat

The design, construction, and materials used for strike camps, as with any fortification, were based on the nature of the threat. The primary threat was considered to be a night assault by light infantry supported by comparatively light crew-served weapons.

In the early days of the war a reinforced VC battalion might be employed against the lightly defended camps. Reinforcements might include sappers and additional crew-served weapons. In later attacks a reinforced VC or NVA regiment would conduct the assault. These later attacks sometimes involved a siege and part of the regiment or other units would be required to secure dominating terrain features such as hilltops, block ground reinforcement routes, and secure nearby helicopter landing zones. A camp siege required significant support from anti-aircraft weapons, as Free World Forces' air power would enter the picture in the form of close air support, airdrop of supplies, and helicopter insertion of reinforcements and relief forces, not just in the camp, but also in adjacent areas. Extensive use was made of transport troops to man-pack ammunition and supplies to the vicinity of the target camp.

An attack was preceded by a thorough reconnaissance of the camp and the surrounding area. Targets for crew-served weapons would be selected and specific weapons assigned to these targets. Key targets were perimeter machine gun bunkers, mortar positions, other crew-served weapons, USSF and LLDB team houses, the tactical operations center, and the communications bunker. Informers inside the camp were sometimes available to provide information. It was not uncommon for at least some VC to have infiltrated a strike force by signing up as CIDG. There were also a few instances where VC sympathizers actively supported the attack from within the camp by knocking out key facilities, weapons, or individuals.

The VC/NVA would also determine the sympathies of local villagers. While most were loyal to the South Vietnamese Government, they could be intimidated to provide information or to cooperate by providing information, food, supplies, guides, man-packing supplies, or simply keeping their mouths shut. Frequently local villagers provided word of an impending attack, having been approached by the VC or witnessed their activities. The VC/NVA also sought information about local patrol routes and schedules, outposts, guard post locations, camp routine, the construction and pattern of barbed wire barriers and other obstacles, mine locations, numbers and types of crew-served weapons, and the locations, possible routes and landing zones that relief forces might utilize.

The attackers would stockpile ammunition and supplies (particularly rations, medical supplies, and water) in the area in hidden caches. Movement routes, assembly areas, attack positions, supporting crew-served weapons locations, and attack points would be reconnoitered and selected. The bulk of the actual attack force would arrive in the area only a short time before the attack in order to reduce the chances of detection. A scale model of the camp was usually prepared to brief the leaders. Rehearsals were conducted, usually in an area a considerable distance from the camp itself.

Defenses against infantry and sapper attacks required multiple dense barbed wire barriers and other obstacles. The effective deployment of machine guns and mortars in mutually supporting positions was essential. While it was necessary to cover all approaches, multiple weapons were also required to cover each sector or approach in the event one or more were knocked out. Regardless

A camp could look extremely rundown and battered. They were never finished, being constantly rebuilt, repaired, and upgraded.

of the density of barriers, the effective emplacement of weapons, fire coordination, and the use of mines and trip flares, the most effective means of defense was constant vigilance.

The design and construction of camps took into consideration the types of weapons the attackers would employ. These were generally relatively light and were seldom employed in large numbers, although there were exceptions when significant numbers of mortars or machine guns, for example, were employed. The supporting weapons employed by the attackers could be divided into five broad categories:

- Machine guns and small arms: these were direct-fire weapons, usually of 7.62mm caliber, but they offered only limited penetration of fortification materials. They were employed for suppressive fire on the perimeter and of course were used in the assault. Protection from sniper fire was a concern at some camps. Machine guns of 12.7mm caliber were also employed and were excellent for providing suppressive fire owing to their greater penetration. However, most of these were reserved for use as anti-aircraft weapons.
- Recoilless rifles and RPGs (rocket-propelled grenades): the most common recoilless rifles were the 57mm and 75mm, either US-made or Chinese copies, along with the Soviet-made 73mm recoilless gun. These weapons achieved relatively light penetration of fortification materials and their terminal effects (inside the fortification) were nominal as their shaped-charge warheads were designed to defeat tanks. The 73mm recoilless gun achieved better penetration, as did the shoulder-fired RPG-2s and RPG-7s, but these were short-range weapons.

- Mortars: 60mm, 82mm, and 120mm mortars were extremely effective fire support weapons and could cause a great deal of damage, especially if delay fuses were available to permit high explosive rounds to penetrate bunker roofs. Mortars were in effect the VC/NVA's artillery. In most instances, prolonged concentrated mortar fire caused the most damage and the majority of casualties within camps.
- Free-flight rockets: 107mm, 122mm, and 140mm unguided rockets were often less than effective when fired at camps; as a result, they were seldom used. Because of the crude expedient launchers from which they were fired they were notoriously inaccurate, and so it was difficult to hit small camps. They proved to be more effective against air bases and larger Free World bases.
- Grenades and demolitions: hand-delivered explosives were carried by sappers and assault troops to enable them to breech obstacles and destroy bunkers and other facilities. Satchel charges, pole charges, and bangalore torpedoes were the types most commonly employed.

The VC/NVA lacked conventional field artillery until near the war's end, so this was not a major concern; nor was air attack. Some consideration was given to the threat of tank attack depending on the camp's location. This was not a major concern in much of the mountainous north or the southern waterlogged Mekong Delta, nor for camps located far from the border. Camps close to the border and on tank-accessible terrain did take precautions and positioned recoilless rifles for anti-tank defense. From 1967, camps in particularly dangerous locations were provided with jeep-mounted 106mm recoilless rifles and additional disposable, shoulder-fired M72 light anti-armor weapons (LAW). In 1968 and 1969 two border camps were attacked by PT-76 light tanks, with one of the camps being overrun.

Most attacks occurred at night, after the inhabitants had turned in. Attacks were seldom launched just before dawn, but around midnight, because the attackers needed the maximum amount of darkness to complete the assault, consolidate, and withdraw from the area. A daylight withdrawal under air attack could be as costly as the attack on the camp itself.

It was a mistake to consider certain areas as unlikely attack routes in the conventional sense. The VC/NVA were just as likely – or even more likely – to attack across an airfield or other open area, from an adjacent river, out of a swamp, or through a shallow flooded area. Some camps made the mistake of assuming that the enemy would not attack from a sector between the camp and a nearby village.

The 71ft radio antenna tower was critical to a camp's survival, linking it with adjacent camps, fire support bases, and its controlling B-team.

Even if a self-defense force protected the village, the enemy would quietly infiltrate the narrow area between the camp and village and attack from that direction.

The design of Special Forces camps evolved as the CIDG Program grew, the camps were deemed more permanent rather than temporary defensive measures, the VC/NVA became more aggressive, additional resources became available to USSF, and enemy capabilities and tactics changed. Factors affecting the design of camps included the nature of the terrain on which they were built, local weather conditions, the availability of local materials, construction resources, and the degree and nature of the threats faced by specific camps.

The early camps in the Central Highlands were considered temporary in nature. It was hoped that an area could be pacified (rid of VC), or at least the local VC capabilities could be sufficiently degraded so that only minimal village self-defense forces were necessary. That is how the early camps were viewed: defensive outposts from which to guard local villages. The early camps initially possessed very light fortifications and minimal obstacles. In many areas the only threats were probes and harassing sniper fire. Often the local VC did not possess the strength or wherewithal to mount an outright attack on even these minimally defended outposts.

In many areas VC capabilities increased as weapons, equipment, and supplies flowed into South Vietnam from North Vietnam via the Ho Chi Minh Trail. With increased capabilities and the fielding of better-trained and more heavily armed VC Main Force units, the enemy grew bolder and attacks on camps became more frequent. In some instances camps were overrun. In response, camps were hardened, denser defenses and inner perimeters were built, strike forces were increased in size, training became more formalized, and additional crew-served weapons were provided.

A significant threat existed in the form of the *Bo Tu Linh Dac Công*, or Special Attack Corps. These "sappers" were specially trained assault and reconnaissance troops. They were trained to infiltrate through barbed wire barriers, cut and mark assault routes, neutralize Claymore mines and trip flares, and attack targets within the camp with demolition charges. Sappers also often conducted much of the pre-assault reconnaissance of camps.

Camp design

The upgraded and hardened camps were termed "fighting camps," the first being Plei Djereng under A-251 located in the Central Highlands. Fighting camps were more than just a base of operations from which to conduct local patrols and protect nearby villages. They were designed to withstand major determined assaults and prolonged sieges, and to provide a launch site for aggressive combat operations in each camp's tactical area of responsibility (TAOR). Ideally, strike companies would operate up to six miles from their camp. This meant that the border camps would, if possible, be positioned 12 miles apart. Because of terrain restrictions and insufficient forces to man all the camps necessary, the average distance between border camps was actually 17 miles, even further in more rugged areas.

It is often said that the best defense is a good offense, and this is no less true for the security of a Special Forces camp. An aggressive plan of combat and reconnaissance operations throughout a camp's TAOR, frequent security patrols around the camp, outposts positioned on key terrain, ambushes established at night on approaches, and favorable relations and a good intelligence net established in local villages did as much to protect the camps as the most formidable defenses.

The concept of the hardened fighting camp came about as a result of a determined VC attack on Camp Nam Dong in I CTZ in July 1964. After a heavy mortar barrage, multiple attacks struck the camp and overran the outer perimeter. The camp held out because it had an inner perimeter containing key facilities and mortar positions. The concept of a well-fortified inner perimeter capable of holding out even if the rest of the camp was overwhelmed became mandatory practice.

The French had built hundreds of small concrete squad pillboxes all over the country to control and secure roads, railroads, intersections, and bridges. Of course, this sort of widely scattered static defense relying on mobile reaction forces failed. They controlled nothing except that which was within range of their machine guns. At night they were on their own as relief forces were easily ambushed and delayed long enough for the little pillboxes to be overrun. Strike camps encountered a similar problem as they were usually located in even more remote areas and nighttime relief was impractical. The camps though were usually of sufficient strength to enable them to hold out until daylight. The pillboxes differed in design, but typically consisted of a circular machine gun pillbox with multiple firing ports and a rectangular compartment for troop quarters. Actually, only a small number of camps used an existing pillbox; most were built in more remote areas, or the position of a pillbox was considered unsuitable for a much larger camp's area.

The designs of the French pillboxes were constantly revised, and designated as *Forces de Terre Sud Viet-Nam* (Ground Forces, South Vietnam – FRSV), followed by the year in which they were introduced. They were individually identified by their *poste kilomètrique*

Camp An Diem was opened in March 1963 and operated by three different A-teams rotating on six-month temporary duty tours. It was closed in July 1964. The early camps were very weakly fortified, often lacking a defined perimeter and even wire barriers, except perhaps for one or two 4–6-strand cattle fences.

RIGHT Thien Ngon, A-323, III CTZ, opened February 1968. This was in the shape of a five-pointed star with broad arms (part of which are cut off) surrounding a large five-sided inner perimeter. The outer perimeter is a high earth berm lined with covered fighting positions and backed by CIDG and dependents' quarters. A circular road surrounds the inner perimeter, with a wire barrier on both sides. The 105mm howitzer platoon position is in the lower right arm. Camp Prek Klok, A-322, was of similar construction.

FAR RIGHT Camp Dong Xoai, A-342, III CTZ, opened May 1965. The irregular rectangular area to the right contains the 105mm howitzers and was probably an existing government compound. The extensive trench system on the outer and inner perimeters was added in 1966. The small barracks were replaced by a smaller number of larger barracks situated perpendicular to the perimeter. While under construction by Seabees the outer perimeter was overrun, but the inner perimeter held.

(kilometer post number – PK) along provincial routes. Little has been documented regarding their design, but Bernard Fall briefly described them in *Street Without Joy* (Stackpole Books, 1964):

"There was the multi-chambered block which appeared in the spring of 1951, followed by the [30ft × 30ft] three-chambered block of the middle of 1951. Then came the round block of the end of 1951, containing a specially protected command chamber in the middle; and the easier-to-build hexagonal block of 1952. In 1953 came the hexagon with a small square attachment, and finally there was the small, squarish block of 1954, with a square attachment … with its armor plate door and porthole covers; its central radio room, measuring 6ft by 4ft (aptly known as 'the tomb')."

"Subsurface fighting camps" were built in areas adjacent to the border as they received such heavy and frequent mortar fire. Katum Camp (known as "Kaboom") in III CTZ was actually used as the training target for an NVA mortar school across the border in Cambodia. All critical facilities and quarters were at least 3ft below ground, with a minimum of 5ft of overhead cover topped by heavily sandbagged fighting bunkers. Heavy revetting and

Camp Gia Vuc, A-103, I CTZ, opened February 1962. Its five-sided perimeter is a raggedly aligned trench with covered fighting positions. The inner perimeter is sprawling and irregularly shaped, as was the case in many of the early camps. It appears that one 105mm howitzer position has been completed and the other (above it) is still under construction. The four wire barriers are completely clear of vegetation. An internet virtual tour of Gia Vuc can be found at: http://www.gia-vuc.com/GIA-VUC-CAMP.htm.

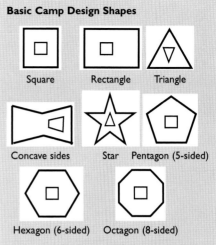

Basic Camp Design Shapes

Square   Rectangle   Triangle

Concave sides   Star   Pentagon (5-sided)

Hexagon (6-sided)   Octagon (8-sided)

Machine gun bunkers were located at each corner or angle and one or more on each straight section of the walls, the total number depending on the length of the wall. All four sides of square or rectangular camps could have concave sides. The inner perimeter was located roughly in the camp's center and could be of any shape, but was usually square or triangular. The equilateral triangular camp has a counter-posed triangular inner perimeter. Triangular camps were sometimes elongated, i.e. an isosceles triangle.

sometimes overhead cover was provided for facilities not normally provided with this protection, such as the camp's truck park.

"Surface fighting camps" were built using sandbags, timber, logs, and some CONEX containers. Another design used 86 CONEX containers for bunkers and quarters.

"Floating fighting camps" were first built in early 1967 in the flood-prone Mekong Delta, the waters of which could rise by 10ft during the wet or monsoon season from April to November. Combat operations were conducted using airboats and sampans, but VC activity was often light during the floods. Facilities were built on pilings, sandbagged berms, or on floating platforms on sealed drums that rose and fell with the water level. Over 500 empty fuel drums were required for each camp. Floating platforms were anchored to pilings by cable loops; when the water level subsided the platform settled on the ground. Mortar positions were built into the tops of high mounds and sandbagged to prevent erosion, or atop flooded-out concrete machine gun bunkers. Once the floodwaters had receded a great deal of maintenance work had to be undertaken to make the camp suitable for dry operations.

In addition to the Strike Force camps, numerous other USSF bases were built along the same lines. These included the B- and C-team camps, defended by a single CIDG company and located in provincial capitals along with other Free World compounds and units. There were also CIDG training camps, MIKE Force bases, special reconnaissance project bases and forward operating bases (FOB), and communication replay sites: all specialized facilities, but defended in much the same way as the strike camps.

Many of the early camps were merely a collection of thatched-roof buildings, some mortar positions, a few perimeter bunkers, some entrenchments, and barely any perimeter obstacles. Some hardly had a defined perimeter; it was often simply a line of lightly constructed bunkers and fighting positions without a connecting trench. The CIDG lived in tents and huts built in the local style. The site of the village or villages they were protecting determined each camp's location. Camps could be built atop hills, on the sides of mountains, on flat plateaus, in a jungle clearing, in valleys (to

Non-standard Concertina Wire Barriers

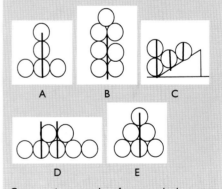

A   B   C

D   E

Cross-section examples of non-standard concertina wire barriers. Horizontal strands on pickets (indicated by vertical lines) and guy wires anchored to short pickets support all examples. A concertina coil is 3ft 4in. in diameter, making B, for example, almost 13ft high. The two addition base coils in A could reinforce any other type of barrier, B or E for example, but might be found only on one side or both. A variation of B was a third row of three stacked coils. C is typical of concertina emplaced on the face of an inner perimeter berm. D was comparatively low, but its width made sapper penetration or bridging by scaling ladder difficult. Both the base and second-layer coils could be made wider. E could also be made wider by adding more base, second- and even third-layer coils.

Conceptual fighting camp layout

This illustration provides a basic conceptual layout of a triangular-shaped strike force camp with a counter-posed inner perimeter. Regardless of a given camp's shape, the same facilities and defensive considerations would be incorporated.

Key:

A. Concertina and barbed wire barriers.
B. Area sewn with tanglefoot wire, Claymore mines, and trip flares.
C. Open area wider than grenade range between inner wire barrier and outer perimeter.
D. Guard hut.
E. Gates. Additional concertina coils block the road between gates.
F. Fuel dump (protected by berm).
G. Trench line with fighting position, either at ground level or atop an earth berm.
H. Helicopter pad.
I. Parade ground.
J. Outer perimeter wall .30-cal. M1919A6 machine gun bunkers (one gun).
K. Outer perimeter corner .30-cal. M1919A6 machine gun bunkers (two guns).
L. Inner perimeter .30-cal. M1919A6 machine gun bunkers (one gun).
M. Inner perimeter berm faced with concertina wire.
N. Lateral compartmentalization wire barriers.
O. 60mm M19 mortar positions.
P. 81mm M29 mortar positions.
Q. .50-cal. M2 machine gun positions (atop bunker).
R. 57mm M18A1 recoilless rifle position (atop bunker).
S. Schoolhouse.
T. Vehicle maintenance shop.
U. Dispensary.
V. Co Lac Bo.
W. Strikers' and dependents' quarters.
1. USSF team house.
2. USSF quarters.
3. LLDB team house and quarters.
4. Supply and arms rooms with interpreters' quarters attached.
5. Communications bunker with radio antenna tower.
6. Power generators.
7. Emergency medical bunker.
8. Ammunition bunkers.

block infiltration), or on delta swamps edging a canal or river. Soil conditions, drainage, nearby key terrain features which could be occupied by the enemy, fields of observation and fire, suitability for an airfield, road access, and even the desires of local government officials and inhabitants were taken into consideration when choosing a site. Occasionally some government officials directed camps to be built on less-than-favorable sites.

By 1968, more-or-less standard designs of buildings were available to include: 20ft × 60ft wood-frame barracks and dependents' quarters; 20ft × 40ft frame buildings for rice storage; supply rooms and other administrative buildings (supply room, arms room, dispensary, school, maintenance building, workshop, mess halls, and others in which personnel were not quartered; their sizes varied); 16ft × 20ft ammunition bunkers; 8ft × 12ft latrines; 8ft × 8ft machine gun bunkers; and 8ft × 12ft fighting and living bunkers. Non-standard designs continued to be constructed though.

The shape of camps varied greatly: square, rectangular, triangular, five-pointed stars, five-, six- or eight-sided, or irregularly shaped to follow terrain contours. One camp was an interconnected series of fortresses built on eight closely spaced hills. Some square, rectangular, or diamond-shaped camps had indented (re-entrant) sides. Some rectangular camps had only the two long sides indented; a polygon-shape. Re-entrant sides allowed defensive fire anywhere along the walls to be easily directed at attackers, even from the far end of the sidewall on attackers at the other end. Some camps had odd-shaped extensions for expansion.

Circular or other freeform or irregularly shaped camps were difficult to defend, and these designs were later avoided. A circular or roughly oval-shaped camp precluded the concentration of defensive fire and forced

Camp Phu Quoc, A-427, IV CTZ, opened February 1965. This little camp was built at the base of a small knoll on its upper side. It has no inner perimeter as such, but the knoll was developed as a stronghold. The outer perimeter is a low sandbag wall with open fighting positions.

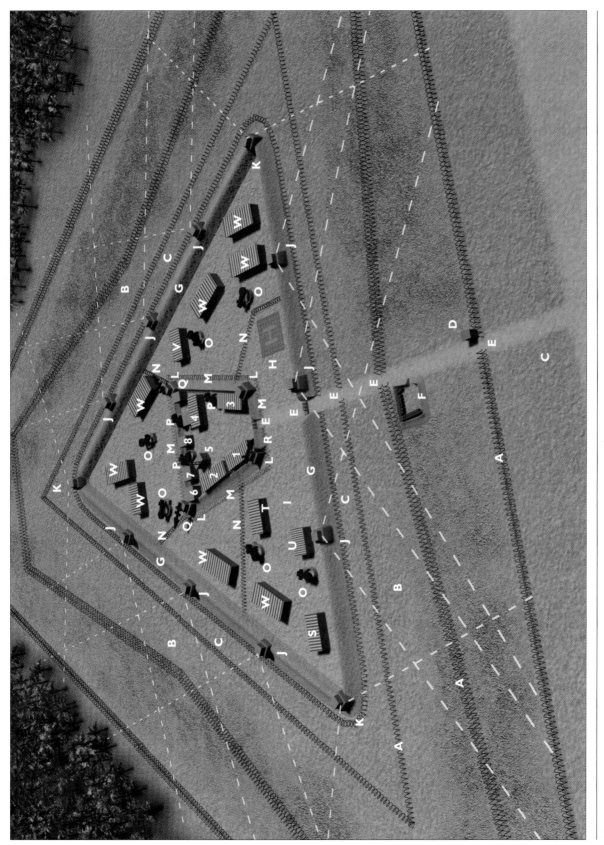

15

machine gun positions to cover wider sectors of fire.

The size of a camp varied depending on its shape, the facilities it would enclose, the size of the Strike Force, the number of dependents it housed, and terrain restrictions, but 490–820ft across was typical. Some camps were much smaller with their facilities and structures tightly packed. Consequently, a mortar round dropped into such camps would hit something. Some camps were so small that there was not enough space for an internal helicopter pad. The obstacle belt could be 330ft or more across.

Most camps housed Strike Force dependents. On the surface this sounds like a less-than-desirable option, but it was better than the alternative of housing families in a nearby village. This led to many Strikers spending nights at home rather than in the camp when attacks were likely and there was a great deal of in-and-out traffic. The increased traffic made it difficult to control exactly who entered the camp, and there were instances where the VC held dependents hostage. Strikers could not be expected to defend the camp with their families in danger. The concept of the CIDG was to recruit locally to defend villages and it was not always an option to separate Strikers from their families. Strikers fought harder and deserted their posts less often when they were defending not only the camp, but also their families. In most cases, dependents living inside the camps posed few problems. A camp typically was home to some 1,000 Strikers and their dependents, making it a small community with all the associated problems and infrastructure required of a small town.

The core of the fighting camp was the inner perimeter, designed to hold out if the outer perimeter collapsed. It contained command and control facilities as well as secured ammunition and supplies, and was the camp's day-to-day nerve center. The USSF and LLDB team houses were here. The USSF team house typically consisted of a common room that served as the radio, meeting and recreation room, and as a general administrative work area. It often contained a bar and a large table. There would be an office or two for the team CO and team

Camp Tong La Chon, A-334, III CTZ, opened March 1967. Most of the later camps were larger, but Tong La Chon was small and cramped. It was later enlarged. When attacked and almost overrun five months after its opening, conditions were so poor only 50 assigned CIDG remained (others had quit). It had to be defended by a company rotated from another camp plus almost 600 MIKE Force. The earth berm outer perimeter is defended by almost 40 fighting and living bunkers, each with its own well-revetted entry trench. Two 105mm howitzers are positioned in the right arm; two 81mm mortars are in the inner perimeter and two in the left arm.

Camp Dan Thanh, A-423, IV CTZ, opened April 1964. This rectangular camp was built at the base of Ap An Nong Hill (115ft above sea level), which was incorporated into the camp. There is both an inner perimeter in the lower camp and a stronghold atop the hill. The outer perimeter is an earth berm with individual fighting positions.

M18A1 Claymore Anti-personnel Mine

Scores and even hundreds of command-detonated Claymore mines surrounded strike camps. The Claymore was a 3½ lb directional mine comprised of a rectangular, slightly curved fiberglass box with 1½ lbs of C4 plastic explosive backing an epoxy matrix in which were embedded 704 steel ball bearings ⁷⁄₃₂in. (approximately 6mm) in diameter. It was electrically detonated by command or it could be rigged with a tripwire to be activated by an intruder.

When detonated the ball bearings were blasted out in a 60-degree fan with an optimum range of 165ft, but they were dangerous out to 820ft. Blast and secondary fragmentation was dangerous within 330ft in all directions. Claymores were devastating to assault troops.

Numerous methods were used to prevent infiltrators from removing or turning Claymores toward the defenders. They could be secured to pairs of short barbed wire pickets driven into the ground, wrapped with barbed wire, set in concrete bases poured into shallow holes, booby-trapped with grenades or trip flares, or the backs could be painted white to help the mine be detected if moved by an infiltrator.

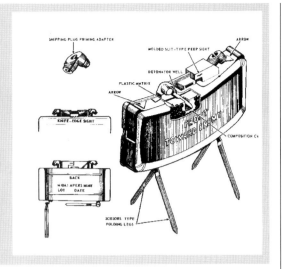

sergeant. A dining area and kitchen were also part of the team house. Team quarters might be a single building or they could be separated, with two- and three-man quarters scattered about the inner perimeter. Officers had their own quarters. The communication sergeants commonly slept in the communications bunker and one or two of the medics might sleep in the emergency medical bunker. The interpreters' and nurses' quarters were also located within the inner perimeter. The TOC and commo bunkers, often combined, were heavily bunkered. The commo bunker or room was air-conditioned to protect the equipment from heat and humidity. A radio antenna tower, as high as 71ft, was mounted beside the commo bunker/TOC. The emergency medical bunker was a protected treatment facility for use if the camp was attacked.

The supply room was essentially a small warehouse holding Striker uniforms, web gear, general supplies, and the CIDG rice supply. There was an arms room where weapons repairs were undertaken and spare weapons stored. A washroom with showers was here as were latrine facilities. Interconnected 55-gallon drums were mounted on the roof to store shower water, though some camps had more elaborate plumbing, even flush toilets and hot water. Two or more ammunition bunkers were within the inner perimeter. This is also where the 81mm and 4.2in mortars were usually positioned. The camp's few vehicles were parked within, typically comprising two 2½-ton M35 cargo trucks, a ¾-ton M37B1 cargo truck, and a ¼-ton M151A1 utility truck (jeep). One or two 400-gallon M149 water trailers ("water buffaloes") were available along with some form of emergency water storage. The trailers were kept filled and were often parked in revetments.

Early camps lacked electrical power except for a small 1.5kW generator for minimal lighting in the inner perimeter, critical lighting in the medical bunker, and to run movie projectors for morale purposes, etc. Gasoline-burning refrigerators were provided for medical supplies and to store radio batteries. Later, most camps had two 10kW generators to supply sufficient power for minimal lighting

Camp Vinh Gia, A-422, IV CTZ, opened August 1964. The outer perimeter was a high trench-topped berm with covered fighting positions and machine gun bunkers. The wide moat was kept filled with water from the canal. The inner perimeter is at the end adjacent to the canal as it was believed that any penetrations would be on the landward side, so it was backed up against the canal. Across the canal is a government-built resettlement village.

Camp Bu Dop, A-341, III CTZ, opened November 1963. This camp originally had a moat. It was extensively rebuilt after attacks in 1967. The zigzag trench has over 20 fighting positions and two machine gun bunkers on each concave wall plus corner bunkers. Most of the barracks and other buildings are sunk to almost ground level. No less than 18 mortar pits can be seen. Several machine gun and/or recoilless rifle positions are inside the upper wall. Two 105mm howitzers occupy the right side while a composite ARVN battery of four 105mm and two 155mm howitzers occupy the left side. Rows of CONEXs are near the inner perimeter gate for additional bunkers.

M49A1 Trip Flare

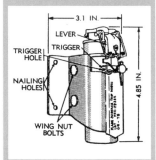

The olive drab-painted M49A1 trip flare was 1½in. in diameter, almost 5in. long, and weighed 15oz. They were attached to barbed wire pickets or stakes by a mounting bracket, or simply wired to a stake without the bracket, several inches above the ground within barrier wire entanglements and rigged to be activated by a tripwire up to 40ft in length. When activated the magnesium flare ignited immediately, burning for 55–70 seconds (60 seconds on average) at 50,000 candlepower at 4,200 °F and illuminating an area up to 985ft in radius.

purposes throughout the camp. Refrigerators, chest-type freezers, and even television sets were available, though programming was limited to the Armed Forces Radio and Television Service (AFRTS) and a couple of Vietnamese stations. A 1.5kW generator was available for emergency back-up purposes. One of the two big diesel 10kW generators ran 24 hours a day; the other "rested" for servicing. Sandbag revetments protected the generators while affording sufficient space around them for servicing and ventilation purposes. Each revetment had a sandbag-covered roof, but with a wide gap in the wall under the eves all around for ventilation. The revetment muffled the noise, but the hum of the generator was constant, eventually becoming an unnoticed background noise.

The inner perimeter wall was usually a berm (the term means the lip or shelf between a parapet and the edge of a trench or moat, but in Vietnam it was the common term for a tamped earth dike used as a protective wall or revetment), sometimes with a trench system or fighting positions. Usually a multiple-coil concertina wire barrier protected the inner perimeter on the berm's face. Machine gun bunkers were positioned at the corners and on each wall, and sometimes the bunkered buildings were incorporated into the inner perimeter walls. The inner perimeter could be square, rectangular, triangular, or of another shape. The triangular-shaped inner perimeter of a triangular-shaped camp was often positioned counter-posed to the outer perimeter, i.e. it pointed the other way.

The Strike Force barracks and dependents' quarters, located in the outer perimeter area, were usually evenly spaced around the perimeter, but in some instances barracks were concentrated in one or two areas. Each company was assigned a perimeter sector. When a company was in the field, elements of another company would take over its perimeter sector. Each company had a small headquarters and in some cases a bunkered command post. Mortar positions (60mm) were spaced around the perimeter.

Numerous facilities were scattered about the outer perimeter: the vehicle maintenance building, dispensary, dependents' school, tailor shop, barber shop, *Co Lac Bo* (combined recreation room and café), and a parade ground which doubled as a helicopter pad if there was no separate pad. In camps too small for an internal helicopter pad, one was usually situated within the barrier wire beside the entry road.

Communications trenches connected certain areas of the camp with the inner perimeter, though some camps lacked these. Besides allowing protected movement about the camp, they were used as lateral defense lines to seal off a portion of the camp that the enemy had penetrated. Lateral barbed wire barriers sometimes divided the outer perimeter area into segments to compartmentalize the camp if penetrated.

Latrines were scattered about the camp, as were 55-gallon water drums for bathing water and firefighting along with sand buckets. Most camps had a water-well, but others required water to be hauled from a nearby source and so possessed additional water storage for emergencies. Burnout-type latrines were employed. These were outhouses with a 55-gallon drum cut down to one-third its height and placed under each toilet seat. When full they were pulled out, diesel fuel was mixed with the waste, and burned. This may sound disagreeable, but it was efficient and sanitary. Urinal tubes ("piss tubes") were situated about the camp. These were 4–6in.-diameter pipes embedded in gravel-filled holes and angled upward, projecting about 2ft out of the ground.

From 1968 onward, many camps were provided with a 105mm howitzer platoon manned either by CIDG or ARVN (sector artillery platoons) gunners, to provide artillery support to Strike Force field operations and to cover areas that were beyond the range of fire support bases. They were emplaced in a small compound of their own adjacent to the inner perimeter. In smaller camps an extension to the outer perimeter had to be added as sufficient internal space for the artillery position did not exist. The artillery area might have its own berm or defenses, but sometimes the position was simply built within the camp with no defined separation. It included two circular sandbagged howitzer positions with attached ammunition bunkers, a separate main ammunition bunker, a small fire direction center bunker, and crew quarters. If manned by ARVN troops, they had their own 2½-ton trucks. In 1969, because of the availability of "beehive" flechette rounds, it was directed that the howitzers be positioned where they could deliver direct fire into at least part of the outer barrier. The guns, however, were emplaced and the effort to reposition them and construct new emplacements was considered to be not worth the effort.

Some camps had a separate administrative area outside the outer perimeter through which the entry road passed, but within the barrier wire. This was common in remote areas where camps were relied upon for government services, the district headquarters being too distant. The position of this separate

Camp Mang Bak, A-246, IV CTZ, opened July 1964. This small camp, like so many of the early ones, follows the contours of a ridge. There is no inner perimeter as such. In the upper portion a large below-ground combined TOC is under construction. The outer perimeter is a high wall with firing ports and machine gun bunkers at key points backed by living bunkers and barracks. A C-7A Caribou transport sits on the partly planked runway. If the runway's soil was sufficiently compacted, only the landing portion required planking.

Punji Stakes

Punji stakes were used extensively as an obstacle at early camps. The bamboo or hardwood stakes were set in the ground at an angle in dense fields between wire belts, in low ground, moats, drainage ditches, and on the front of berms.

Punji stakes were 12–18in. long and sharpened on both ends, allowing them to be pushed 5–6 in. into the ground. The end was char-hardened to increase the chance of it penetrating a boot sole.

Ideally they were placed in clusters of three, one angled forward about 45 degrees and the other two angled at about 30 degrees to the right and left. Their manufacture was time-consuming, especially if char-hardened. They deteriorated over time, were destroyed when brush was burned, and as more concertina became available they were seldom replaced.

Punji stakes (and the name) originated in the Punjab region of northwest India, and are of ancient origin. Their use in

jungle warfare was discussed in a British intelligence report in 1944, reprinted in a US intelligence publication later that same year. These traps eventually appeared in US Army Special Forces manuals in the 1950s and the South Vietnamese used them early in the conflict to defend camps and villages as a substitute for then scarce barbed wire. The VC subsequently used them as well, especially along side trails on which ambushes were established, in concealed small *punji* trap holes on trails, and to defend base camps.

administrative area, which contained the dispensary for local civilians and Vietnamese government agency assistance offices, prevented unauthorized civilians from entering the camp proper. These facilities were occupied only during daylight and were closed off from the camp at night. The fuel dump was located outside the outer perimeter, but inside the barrier wire near the road. The gasoline and diesel fuel drums and oil drums were protected by an earth berm or barrier made of soil-filled drums without overhead cover.

Kinh Quan II, A-412, IV CTZ, opened October 1965. KQ II is still under construction in this photo. The outer berm is lined with temporary fighting and living bunkers, but with few on the river side. Buildings inside the inner perimeter are still under construction. The inner perimeter is unique in that it possesses a moat. It appears the camp was built over an existing fortification.

Camp Chi Linh, A-333, opened January 1967, was originally known as Cau Song Ba. Compare this photo to the camp diagram on page 21. The USSF team house (the V-shaped building) had its team quarters (the upper arm) destroyed by fire. The drainage ditches outside the outer perimeter are actually shallower and narrower than they appear and choked with concertina wire. This was the author's camp.

There might be a similar, but much smaller and well-protected dump inside the camp with a few fuel drums for ready use by trucks and generators.

The outer barrier could be up to 330ft or more across. This band of barbed wire obstacles was referred to simply as "the wire" and consisted of multiple belts of different types of concertina and barbed wire obstacles. A "belt" was a line of any type of wire. A "band" consisted of two or more belts emplaced in depth with no significant distance between the belts. Patterns and the types of barriers employed varied greatly. Tanglefoot, a zigzag line of loose or taut barbed wire on stakes about 1ft high, was often placed between belts. The idea was to trip attackers as they rushed forward and to hinder infiltrators.

U-shaped, olive drab-painted steel barbed wire pickets were available in 24, 36, 60, and 96in. lengths, generally called 2, 3, 5, and 8ft pickets. The open "U" side of the picket should face the enemy. Wooden posts were often used in the early days, but they deteriorated rapidly and were easier to breach with explosives.

Standard barbed wire was issued in reels weighing 91½ lbs and measuring 1,312ft. Concertina wire is a coiled spool of barbed wire that can be stretched out or collapsed back into a roll for recovery and reuse. Prefab spring-steel concertina wire with ¾in.-long barbs was introduced at the end of World War II. Prefab concertina rolls were 3ft 4in. in diameter, about 50ft long when extended, and weighed 55 lbs. Barbed tape concertina was adopted in the early 1960s and was increasingly issued as the old concertina wire was used up. Although its dimensions were the same, a roll weighed only 31 lbs. It was also sharper and more difficult to cut. Barbed tape was also issued on various-sized spools in lieu of standard barbed wire.

The most basic wire fence was the four-or-more strand "cattle fence" on 4–6ft pickets. The cattle fence was the basis for more elaborate entanglements. The double-apron fence, for example, was a cattle-fence with anchor wires in a "V" pattern on both sides. Across the anchor wires on both sides were placed horizontal strands that formed a sloping barrier, the aprons. A high wire entanglement is two parallel "cattle fences" about 10ft apart with the pickets staggered. A zigzag fence of four or more strands connects the two rows of alternating pickets. Any combination of these entanglements, usually reinforced with concertina wire, could be used to construct bands of barbed wire obstacles. Because of the need for higher and denser barriers, non-standard entanglements were common. These included multiple rows and layers of concertina wire stacked three or four coils high, supported by horizontal strands on pickets and barbed wire guy lines.

Two to six belts of wire were erected around camps in geometric patterns. While the main belts could be supplemented by intermediate belts, the spaces between belts would have tanglefoot, *punji* stakes, small barbed wire mats to discourage crawling infiltrators, tripwired Claymore mines, trip flares, and grenades fitted with tripwires. Besides tripwire-activated Claymores, command-detonated Claymores were emplaced, often in banks of 4–6 mines at 33ft intervals. The electric firing devices were located in the trenches, often with several firing lines run to one point with the firing devices hanging in clusters. The firing wire would run to one mine, the rest being connected by detonating cord (detcord). When one mine was electrically fired the others would detonate instantly – a "wave-breaker."

The use of tripwire-activated Claymores and grenades or other types of booby-trapping devices gradually fell from use. All too often they were detonated by animals, hard rains and winds, or accidentally by work crews. Tripwired Claymores, grenades, and trip flares had to be deactivated to allow crews to repair and improve wire and cut weeds and brush. This was a hazardous undertaking in its own right, as was reactivating them. They had to be removed entirely, inspected, and replaced when brush within the wire was burned. Buried anti-personnel land mines saw very little use for the same reasons. Small M14 "toe-popper" anti-personnel mines were emplaced in the wire of some early camps. This proved impractical: vegetation would soon take over the wire, but the mines themselves made it almost impossible to clear-cut or burn the vegetation and make repairs to the wire. They also required periodic replacement because of weather deterioration and washouts after heavy rains.

It was a constant battle to control vegetation in the wire, which was difficult to cut because of the density of the barriers, guy wires, tanglefoot, tripwires, and other obstacles. Because of the country's tropical climate, vegetation grew startlingly fast and the lush green growth was very difficult to burn, even when soaked with gasoline.

A plan of Camp Chi Linh, A-333, III CTZ, September 1969. Buildings marked A are troop and dependents' quarters, sunk about 2ft below ground with two-layer-thick sandbag walls and roofs of two layers of sandbags topped by corrugated sheet metal. Buildings marked with an asterisk (*) are also sunken. Arrows at the perimeter bunkers indicate the principal direction of fire and number of machine guns. The perimeter was a concrete-capped parapet with firing ports backed by a shallow trench.

The camp's inner perimeter was defined by an earth berm fronted with four coils of concertina wire. The interior face was revetted by corrugated sheet metal. Buildings marked with an asterisk are either sunken or completely underground. The USSF quarters had burned down in February 1969 and were in the process of being rebuilt. A large TOC was also under construction. The corner bunkers housed one or two machine guns. Bunkers 2, 4, and 6 had a 57mm recoilless rifle on top; bunker 3 had a roof-mounted .50-cal. machine gun. (Richard Hook)

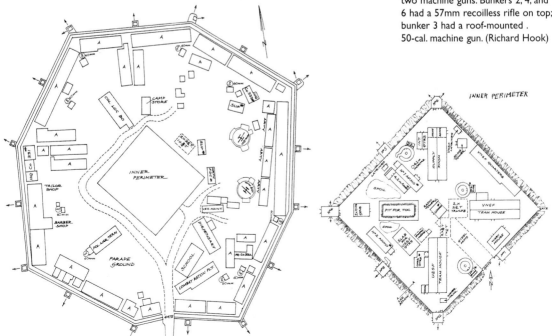

ABOVE LEFT Camp Binh Thanh Thon, A-413, IV CTZ, opened May 1965. This small camp is still under construction in this photo. While two CIDG barracks have been completed most of the troops are still housed in tents. All mortars are contained in the comparatively large inner perimeter. Its design is less than desirable as it has four very wide openings in its berm. This was probably corrected at a later date. The wire barriers are still being installed.

ABOVE RIGHT Camp Cai Cai, A-412, IV CTZ, opened April 1965. The early camp had barracks on each wall and a large administrative building between the combined team house complex. The 1965 flood seriously damaged the original barracks and smaller barracks on 4ft concrete block stilts replaced these. The old administrative building was torn down and replaced by a two-story fortified TOC in the open end of the central complex. One of its wings was provided with a second story for occupation during flooding. During the 1966 flood, with the river 12ft above normal level, temporary hoochs were built atop the barracks. It was soon after this that the camp was modified as a floating camp. The team's designation was changed to A-431 in June 1967.

Camps did not possess perimeter lighting systems because they required too much electrical power, excessive system maintenance, and would have benefited the attacker by allowing him to see perimeter positions and target them as well as clearly see the barriers and obstacles. It was better to keep them in the dark, so to speak.

Moats were utilized at some early camps. They required a good deal of effort though, were difficult to maintain over a prolonged period, and generally fell from use in later camps. They could have a triangular or square cross-section. Dimensions varied, but an 8ft depth and width was considered ideal; many were smaller. Usually, moats only contained water during the wet season. As attackers could shelter in moats, it was essential that they be filled with concertina wire and/or *punji* stakes. To hamper the use of scaling ladders, dense wire entanglements were erected on both sides. Moats were crossable, but the attacker had to make extensive provisions.

Camps had only one gate, usually on the side facing the airfield. The entry road was not necessarily a weak point and attackers more often than not avoided it. Most roads ran straight through the barrier belts and into the camp. Others had one or more sharp turns, this being a more desirable alternative. Multiple machine guns, Claymores, and often at least one recoilless rifle provided covering fire on the road. There were three or more gates constructed of timber or steel framing, densely woven with barbed wire. These were chained shut and tripwired with grenades, Claymores, and trip flares. Barbed wire knife rests (Spanish riders) and multiple coils of concertina wire were pulled across the road between the gates when closed at night and likewise wired to Claymores. Often the road entered the camp onto a parade ground or other open area devoid of cover and covered by inner perimeter machine guns. Some camps had a few narrow zigzag lanes through obstacle belts to allow patrols passage and work parties access to the barriers. These too were blocked with concertina and wired with Claymores and trip flares.

Most camps possessed an airfield, but some in the mountains and the Mekong Delta lacked this facility. They did possess a helicopter pad though. Some were reachable by road, but many in the remote mountains lacked even this and in the Delta the wet season inundated them. Some mountain camps received their supplies routinely by parachute drop. Most airfields could accept a four-engine C-130 transport, requiring them to be 2,500–3,500ft long. One or two turnaround and unloading pads were provided. A fixture at many camps was at least one aircraft hulk resting beside the runway. There was usually a nearby rifle range for the zeroing of weapons and a demolition pit where captured and deteriorating munitions were destroyed.

Occasionally a US fire support base was temporally established near a camp, either at one end of the airfield or adjacent to the camp wire. Defensive fire and local security patrols would be coordinated between the camp and the firebase.

Camp construction

A variety of units and organizations built the strike camps, depending on their location and when they were built. An engineer detachment (539th Engineer Detachment from 1962–67, 31st Engineer Detachment from 1967–70) was assigned to Special Forces to perform technical and service support with four civic action advisory teams (KB teams) and two well-drilling teams (GJ teams). Additional and more technical construction tasks, especially those involving utilities (electrical, water, sewage, drainage) were carried out by civilian engineers and construction crews of Eastern Construction Company, Inc., a contracted Filipino firm. Vietnamese construction firms were contracted if the work was near urban areas.

The engineer detachment provided the 5th SFGA Staff Engineer and assistant staff engineers assigned to each Special Forces company, plus a works and utility section at the group headquarters. The detachment, with 50 or fewer Americans, was involved in the construction and maintenance of the 125 camps constructed from 1962 onward. The five-man KB teams, each of which possessed some heavy equipment, would stay at a new camp site long enough to train the Strikers to construct at least one of each type of building, barracks, bunker, mortar and machine gun position, trench section, and the different types of wire obstacles. The strike force would complete much of the task while working in rotation, some companies working while others conducted local security. The A-team assigned to the camp learned how to operate the heavy equipment under the tutorage of the KB team and its own engineers, and lent a hand as well as supervised. MIKE Force companies were often deployed to provide additional security, but not labor. KB teams also assisted with rebuilding destroyed structures after attacks and upgrading camps. Three-man well-drilling teams could drill and case water wells up to 1,500ft deep.

Naval construction battalion Seabee technical assistance teams (STAT) were also employed. These 13-man teams performed similar jobs to the KB teams, but could also drill wells and possessed additional heavy equipment. US Army

BELOW LEFT A Navy Seabee offloads a light bulldozer from a tilt-bed trailer. Seabee technical assistance teams (STAT) constructed a number of Special Forces camps in the mid-1960s. A 400-gallon M149 water trailer (camps usually had two) is in the background.

BELOW RIGHT A 31st Engineer Detachment KB team member excavates a weapon position with a John Deere bulldozer mounting a backhoe.

Not only local materials were employed, but local transport systems as well. It was the free hand given by Special Forces and the initiative and imagination of SF soldiers that made it all work.

Members of the 5th Special Forces Group Command Readiness Team inspect the condition of a fighting/living bunker. The CRT visited every camp about twice a year to ensure standards were being met and to recommend improvements from lessons learned visiting other camps.

combat engineer companies were sometimes assigned construction missions, particularly if rapid completion was necessary. The Strikers still provided most of the unskilled labor, while the KB and GJ teams assisted. It usually required 4–6 months to complete a camp, although for all practical purposes they were never completed. New construction, upgrading, and repairs were continuous.

While considerable resources were expended to build a camp, there were never enough materials, especially dimensioned lumber, plywood, cement, and chain-link fencing. It was even more difficult to obtain additional materials for subsequent expansion, improvements, and repairs. When camps were closed they were not simply abandoned or razed, but dismantled, even to the point of emptying thousands of sandbags. As much of the building materials as possible was recovered and airlifted out by helicopters or cargo transports, carried by trucks to a new camp site, or distributed to other camps needing improvements, repairs, or expansion. Consequently many substitute and expedient materials and methods were employed. Scrounging and what was called "midnight requisition" were common, but there was a distinct difference between these two widespread and essential practices.

Scrounging was a form of barter, so to speak. Items and materials were usually traded – supply and demand – for goods or services in kind or, sometimes, simply given if there was a surplus. Such exchanges were usually of expendable goods such as construction materials. Accountable items, that is, anything with a serial number, were seldom traded; but it could happen as accountability in Vietnam was sometimes haphazard. Even weapons and vehicles were occasionally traded. Every A-team had one or two individuals who excelled at scrounging. It was even informally taught during Special Forces training. In fact, Special Forces had a well-earned reputation for scrounging and a rather cavalier attitude with regard to property accountability and midnight requisition, the latter often being conducted in broad daylight.

Midnight requisition might be considered outright theft, but it was seldom the case that the offenders, if they were pursued at all, suffered for their transgressions. It was, after all, a unit's responsibility to safeguard its equipment and *matériel*. If it was "barrowed" without permission by another unit, it was the unit's fault for failing to properly secure it. Many felt that the US Army procured only 80–90 percent of what it needed in equipment, repair parts, and *matériel* and that what it had was constantly shifted about between units attempting to make up for shortages. The difference between unauthorized requisition and theft was actually not so fine a line. Midnight requisition was for the benefit of the unit and thus the Army. The *matériel* remained within the Army and was not for personal use or gain. Theft, the subsequent black market sale, and the lining of one's pockets with ill-gotten money from the sale of government property were entirely different matters and would be severely punished.

Most construction materials were requisitioned through normal supply channels, purchased locally from Vietnamese vendors (emphasis was placed on improving the Vietnamese economy through local purchases), or by utilizing available natural resources.

Construction materials

Cement was issued in 94 lb paper sacks. Most was procured from other Asian countries while some was produced in Vietnam's Delta region. Sand and gravel had to be acquired locally in most cases; it was seldom transported into remote locations. Sand was generally only available in the coastal areas and loose gravel too was scarce, so substitutes often had to be found. Sometimes, if areas of suitable rock existed, construction units set up portable gravel crushers. If suitable rock was not available, laterite was often used as a substitute for both sand and gravel. Very common in the Tropics and found in many areas of Vietnam, laterite is a reddish-brown hard clay soil with a high content of iron oxide. It is created from weathered rock with the silica leached out by water passing through where good drainage conditions exist. Once broken up, laterite has a coarse, gravel-like texture.

When used in the production of concrete in Vietnam, laterite required a higher percentage of cement than normal sand and aggregate mixtures and was less resistant to weathering and wear. However, when sprayed with water and rolled it compacted well and was very durable, so it was also used for surfacing airfields,

Camp Plei Do Lim, II CTZ, opened April 1962. Because of difficulties with the LLDB, the new commander of A-334 named it Camp Hardy after CPT Herbert F. Hardy, Jr., killed in action during April 1964. Naming strike camps after Americans was extremely rare and this may have been the only instance. C-team camps, though, were sometimes named in honor of an American. This view displays the outer perimeter sandbag wall faced with PSP and various types of firing ports. The wire barrier comprises two rows of double-stacked concertina. A six-strand cattle fence is set 2ft outside the wall.

Cutaway view of a .30-cal. M1919A6 machine gun bunker on the outer perimeter

The design and dimensions of perimeter machine gun bunkers were as varied as those of the camps they protected. This example represents a typical design dug into the ground and connected to the perimeter trench by a narrow entryway. The interior sides may or may not have been revetted by sandbags, depending on the stability of the soil. The sandbag walls are two layers thick. In this example only sandbags support the roof; it would have been better to provide vertical support beams. Hardened laterite or cement-stabilized sand-filled bags could provide sufficient support though. The firing port is constructed of 2in. × 10in. planks. Seldom were side-firing ports provided except in larger multi-gun corner bunkers. The speed pallet roof (PSP and corrugated steel were also used) is supported by 4in. × 4in. stringers and topped by at least two layers of sandbags. The whole of the exterior is capped with 1–2in. of concrete to protect the sandbags from weather and wear. The guard post is simply constructed of sandbags with a corrugated steel roof to protect the sentry from sun and rain. The machine gun platform is built of sandbags; much more durable and stable than one built of planks. The standard perimeter defense machine gun was the Browning .30-cal. M1919A6 mounted on an M2 tripod.

The gun weighed 32½ lbs, the tripod 14 lbs. Its rate of fire was 450 rounds per minute. A few M1919A4s were also used. The M1919A6 differed in the addition of a flash suppressor, bipod, carrying handle, lighter barrel, and metal shoulder stock (frequently removed). Although the bipod was not used on this bunker gun, it was retained as it helped radiate heat that built up from prolonged firing. The 20–30 ammunition cans typically stowed in the bunker each held a 250-round disintegrating metallic linked belt with one tracer to four ball rounds. The gun was normally protected from the effects of dust by a canvas cover draped over it.

helicopter pads, and roads. Care had to be taken when analyzing laterite because what looked like laterite gravel might simply have been hard, broken-up laterite soil pellets. Mistakenly judging it to be gravel and using it as a roadbed could lead to disaster. A heavy rain could dissolve the pellets, which were not gravel, and turn the road into a sea of mud.

Because of its weight and the amount required for large construction projects, and the limited space available on transport aircraft, cement was used in relatively limited quantities in remote camps. Reinforcing rods (rebar) were seldom used, although 5ft-wide, 150ft-long rolls of steel reinforcing mesh (remesh) with 6in.-square ⅛in.-diameter mesh were sometimes used. Scrap metal, heavy gauge wire, and steel barbed wire pickets were sometimes used as reinforcing, as was barbed wire woven into mesh-like mats.

The outer perimeter sandbag parapet is faced with corrugated sheet metal held in place by steel pipes anchored with barbed wire. Small wood-framed firing ports are provided and each firing step has overhead cover.

Much of the dimensioned lumber in Vietnam was cut locally and purchased from the Vietnamese, or came from elsewhere in Southeast Asia or the Philippines. Rough-cut (unplaned) hardwoods and softwoods were cut in standard plank and timber sizes such as 1in. × 4in., 1in × 6in., 2in. × 4in., 2in. × 8in., 2in. × 10in., 4in. × 4in., 8in. × 8in., etc. Dimensioned lumber was a valuable commodity in Vietnam, as was plywood. The latter, in ¼ and ½in.-thick sheets measuring 4ft × 8ft, was mostly used for building interior walls and as hinged drop-type window covers. Wood, however, deteriorates rapidly in tropical climates, which is why the French installed concrete power and telephone poles and used concrete railroad ties.

Locally cut logs were used to some extent, especially in early camp construction, but because they were not dried they deteriorated even more rapidly. A problem encountered in areas that saw heavy combat was that the trees were riddled with artillery fragments, which damaged saws. Rubber trees were poor for construction purposes. If cut during the dry season, they were dry and brittle; during the wet season the sap was a mess and stank. Tough and resilient bamboo was sometimes used as a construction material, especially in the early days.

Camp Bu Dop. A US 175mm gun battery established in an adjacent temporary fire support base opens fire. In the foreground is the camp's concrete-capped, sandbag-revetted perimeter trench with sandbag-covered individual fighting positions.

Logs of ⅜in. diameter were extensively used to revet walls and trenches. They could be placed vertically or horizontally, but in the latter case vertical support posts were necessary and steel barbed wire pickets were often used. Anchor wires helped support timber revetment walls. Log crib walls, constructed from horizontally laid logs, were built with 2–3ft of soil between the parallel retaining walls that varied in height. These were used as revetments and anti-sniper walls.

Vietnam had possessed a well-developed rail system in the more populated areas, mainly to serve the rubber industry, but the VC had cut most of the lines and blown the bridges. If a Special Forces camp was anywhere near a rail line some of the rail was recovered and used as stringers for bunker roofs. In 1969, when the US was making major efforts to reopen some of the rail lines, a directive was sent down to A-teams instructing them to cease the practice. The longer U-shaped barbed wire pickets were sometimes used as closely spaced roof stringers, if they were not bearing heavy loads.

Galvanized or zinc-coated corrugated sheet metal was extensively used for roofing; in fact it was just about the only roofing material available. Locally made palm thatching was used in some instances, especially in the early camps, but it was very prone to catching fire. Standard corrugated metal had ⅞in.-deep corrugations with 2½in. spacing between the "hills and valleys." The sheets were usually 26in. wide and 8ft long, but longer lengths were also used. Width-wise, corrugated metal was considered too flexible to be used to support revetted walls. It occasionally was, but it required a large number of closely spaced support stakes.

Sandbags were of course extensively used for fortifications. They were made of either light olive green, brown or tan (faded to off-white) burlap, or dull green woven plastic which began to appear in about 1968. The plastic bags were much more durable than the cloth sandbags, which began to deteriorate after a month but which were still issued. Empty sandbags measured 14in. × 26½in. and had a length of tie-cord tacked 3in. from the opening. Sandbags were three-quarters filled and tied close with a square knot. A filled bag weighed 40–75 lbs depending on the soil and moisture content. Average weight with dry sand was 65 lbs. A filled bag measured approximately 4¾in. × 10in. × 19in. Two layers of sandbags provided protection from small arms fire and fragmentation. Gravel-filled sandbags provided almost twice the protection offered by sand-filled sandbags and three times that of sandbags filled with soil. Sandbags were sometimes filled with stabilized sand (two-thirds sand, one-third cement), a mix that solidified after wetting and which was more durable.

A great deal of use was made of various shipping materials and containers for construction. In peacetime, shipping containers were usually required to be turned in for reuse as they were expensive but durable enough for repeated use. In Vietnam, they were seldom returned because of the difficulties of back-haul, transportation shortages, and the urgent need for construction materials. Occasionally directives would be issued requiring that certain containers be returned because of shortages, but these were frequently ignored or just enough were returned to keep higher headquarters happy, the bulk being retained for construction purposes.

Wooden ammunition boxes, especially larger boxes for mortar and artillery rounds, were disassembled for their hinges, latches, and pinewood planks. The planks were useful for shelves, furniture, and other fixtures. Ammunition boxes were also filled with soil and stacked brick-like for revetting, much like sandbags, though the boxes were more durable. They had to be braced by picket posts as a heavy explosion could collapse an ammunition box wall; they did not have the friction of stacked sandbags to hold them in place.

Wooden shipping pallets were also disassembled for their hardwood planks, or were used as flooring in bunkers. A standard pallet measured 40in. × 48in.

and included 5in.-high wooden skids to allow them to be lifted by forklifts. Ammunition boxes and other materials were secured to pallets by steel strapping and delivered to camps. To deliver miscellaneous supplies in cardboard boxes and other small containers, a pallet box made of framed plywood was used. This was the length of two pallets: 40in. wide × 40in. deep. These too were disassembled for reuse.

"Speed pallets" (see page 28 box) were supposed to be returned on a later outbound cargo transport, but more often they became a roof for bunkers covered by sandbags. While the pallets could bear a heavy load when supported, they offered poor resistance to high-impact blows such as mortar rounds and had to be well supported by stringers. The most-frequent calls for return concerned speed pallets, which were costly and often in short supply.

An especially dense razor-wire concertina belt. While providing a formidable obstacle, the difficulties involved in controlling the growth of vegetation can be seen. Some camps sprayed motor oil or asphaltic cutback in an effort to reduce growth, but over time the weeds would still take root. Wire tended to ensnare a lot of blowing waste paper.

Steel drums for 55 gallons of gasoline or diesel were extensively used to construct anti-sniper walls, bunkers, and revetments. The tops were cut off and the 35in.-high, 23in.-diameter drums filled with earth, preferably tamped solid in layers. The drums were typically painted olive green or black, but other colors were used. Another use for drums involved both ends being cut out, the drum cut lengthwise, and flattened out to provide a 35in. × 72in. steel sheet for revetting walls.

Powder bag shipping containers for 155mm, 175mm, and 8in. artillery pieces were olive green heavy gauge steel tubes with an interrupted-tread cap on one end. They were sometimes filled with tamped soil and emplaced vertically; with the bottom ends dug several inches into the ground, to face trench parapets as bullet deflectors. They were also used as drainage pipes with the bottom ends cut out or numerous holes punched in the bottom and the tubes welded end-to-end. The two most common sizes for 155mm cans were 6½in. diameter, 28in. long and 5in. diameter, 42in. long.

Pierced steel planks (PSP; also known as "Marston matting," though this term had fallen from general use by the time of Vietnam) and M8A1 lightweight steel landing matting were used as revetting and sometimes as bunker roofing. Korean War PSP was replaced by M8A1 planking as remaining stocks were used up. As with the speed pallets, sufficient stringers were necessary to support sandbag-covered matting. PSP measured 15in. × 10ft; M8A1 matting was 17½in. × 11ft 9¾in. with four reinforcing ribs running its length. Both types had tabs and slots to allow them to be fastened together and were painted olive drab. Unless a camp's airfield was built on very unstable or soft soil, matting was not used. Rolled and compacted laterite was preferred.

CONEX shipping containers were used as storage lockers and all sorts of bunkers ranging from ammunition storage to quarters to machine gun emplacements. CONEXs were often used as A-team quarters, being just the right size for a two-man room. They were dug in and bunkered, often in two parallel rows with a corridor running down the center and an entrance at both ends.

Corrugated metal pipe (CMP) halves measuring 1–6ft in width and 2ft in length were widely used. The half-sections had a flange along each edge and bolt holes to fasten two halves together; and they were nestable to reduce shipping space. The wider heavy gauge steel halves (arches) were used for bunker and shelter roofs and covered with sandbags as well as drainage and culvert pipes.

CONEX Containers

CONEX (CONtainer EXpress) containers were large, heavy gauge steel boxes for shipping bulk supplies aboard ships and cargo aircraft. The most commonly seen CONEX was 88in. wide, 108in. long (the same dimensions as a speed pallet) and 90in. high with double doors on one end. The olive drab-painted containers were waterproof and extremely robust with ribbed walls.

Two- and three-cell cinder blocks as well as solid concrete blocks were used for some construction, especially team houses, quarters, and other above-ground structures. They were also used extensively for all types of construction in the Delta, as the perpetually wet environment was particularly hard on wood. Molds were available to make the blocks on-site. Standard two-cell blocks measured 8in. × 8in. × 16in. Once the wall was constructed the cells could be filled with sand for increased ballistic protection.

Chain-link fencing (hurricane or cyclone fence) provided protection from RPG fire. It was erected vertically 20–25ft in front of a bunker on pickets; sometimes much closer because of unfamiliarity with the necessary standoff distance. Approximately half of the rockets fired during tests directly struck a fence strand and detonated, causing only superficial blast and fragmentation damage to the bunker's exterior. With the other rockets the nose entered a gap in the strands, the warhead's body made contact with the fence, the piezoelectric fuse shorted out and failed to detonate, and the warhead broke up. Half-inch wire mesh and chicken wire were sometimes used to cover machine gun firing ports to prevent hand grenades and satchel charges from being thrown in.

Construction principles

Construction and the degree of protection applied to different buildings varied greatly from camp to camp. Individual initiative and preferences, the degree of the threat, available materials, terrain conditions, who built the camp, and practices in use at the time of construction determined a given camp's design and construction.

The various administrative buildings were usually of wood-frame construction: concrete slabs or wood-deck floors, horizontal plank walls supported by 2in. × 4in. framing, and corrugated steel roofs supported by 2in. × 6in. stringers. Occasionally the walls might be made of corrugated steel. Team houses and most administrative buildings had exterior waist- or chest-high protected walls made up of sandbags or soil-filled 55-gallon drums.

Team, troop, and dependents' quarters might be wood frame as well, but were more often constructed as bunkers either above ground, semi-sunk (2–4ft below ground), or completely below ground and provided with two- to four-layer sandbag roofs. Roof supports and beams were usually 8in. × 8in. timbers walled with 2in.-think planks.

It was essential that all personnel slept under at least two layers of sandbags for mortar protection. Some camps, however, only had wood-frame living quarters or split bamboo (rattan) and thatched-roof houses based on Montagnard long houses for dependents, but they also provided large bunker shelters. Others were built in the style of log cabins with horizontal logs. Some dependents would even shelter in ammunition bunkers if the camp was attacked. Dependents' housing was often inadequate in the early camps.

Whether bunkered facilities were located above ground, semi-sunk, or below ground depended on the water table, seasonal flooding,

Moats protected some early camps, but they proved to be ineffective given the effort expended to build and maintain them. They could be easily crossed by scaling ladders and even provided attackers with a degree of cover.

construction resources, hardness of the soil, and the indirect fire threat. Below-ground structures were seldom completely buried, their overhead cover being flush with the ground. Commonly the ceiling would be flush with ground level, with the overhead cover above ground. Below-ground or semi-sunken bunkers were often provided with a corrugated steel roof positioned inches above the overhead cover and extending at least a foot beyond. This detonated mortar rounds, prevented rain leakage, and prolonged the life of the sandbags.

The tactical operations center (TOC), communications bunker, and emergency medical bunker (sometimes the first two were combined) were typically completely underground and heavily protected. The two or three ammunition bunkers were similarly protected. In more developed camps there might be an inner perimeter complex with USSF and LLDB team houses, TOC, main dispensary, and other facilities in a single compartmentalized building.

The design and size of perimeter machine gun bunkers varied greatly. They were usually semi-sunk, although some were positioned above ground for the reasons noted above or to obtain a better spread of fire by mounting the weapon higher. There was usually only one firing port per machine gun; seldom were alternate ports provided. Most bunkers mounted a single machine gun, but two or three might be mounted in large corner bunkers to cover multiple sectors of fire. An attached sleeping compartment might be connected to or be part of the bunker. Often a guard post was built atop the bunker, comprising a low sandbag wall with a corrugated steel roof on posts for sun protection.

A USSF officer walks the outer perimeter road (few camps had this feature) between the outer perimeter and wire belts. About 3ft in front of the concrete-capped parapet is a five-strand cattle fence backed by a coil of concertina. Covered fighting positions top the parapet.

The Camp (Trai) Tinh Bien gate in IV CTZ. The guard hut is to the left. At night the gates were closed and multiple concertina coils blocked the road.

Strikers are taught how to operate a Cinva-Ram concrete-brick-making machine. The simple machine was invented in Colombia in the 1950s and introduced into Vietnam by the Seabees. The ram compressed the cement with 1,800 lbs per square inch, precluding the need for gravel aggregate.

The most common type of machine gun bunker consisted of a chest-deep rectangular hole revetted with sandbags and an above-ground sandbag wall at least two layers thick. They could be of any size, with interior dimensions of 5ft × 5ft or larger. The firing port was normally framed with 2in. × 10in. or similar-sized lumber, but sometimes the port was merely faced with sandbags with planks, M8A1 matting, or a speed pallet supporting the overhead sandbags. A stacked sandbag or timber platform was provided for the tripod-mounted machine gun. A narrow door opened directly into the perimeter trench and was usually covered only by a canvas curtain. This was a common weakness of bunkers of all types. They also sometimes lacked protective walls outside the entrance or had entry trenches leading straight into the bunker without a 90-degree turn.

A major problem experienced with bunkers was the failure to support the roof with vertical beams embedded in the ground. If the only form of support was provided by laying stringers across the top of the sandbag walls, the roof would eventually settle or collapse. This was sometime blamed on plastic sandbags as they were "slippery," but in fact it was simply because earth-filled sandbags shifted and settled and could collapse with age or the effects of water absorption. Roofs were supported by 4in. × 4in. timber or log stringers on which was laid corrugated steel, PSP or M8A1 matting, wood planks, or a speed pallet. Tarpaper or plastic sheeting might be used for waterproofing, followed by the desired layers of sandbags. Ideally the whole of the bunker would be capped with a 1–2in. layer of concrete, as applied to many other bunkers and weapon positions. This thin layer of non-reinforced concrete added little ballistic protection, but served to protect the sandbags from wear, weathering, and water absorption. Repeated water absorption and the subsequent drying of a sandbag structure led to its eventual deterioration and the necessity to rebuild it. By contrast, a concrete-capped structure could last for several years. Sandbags were sometimes coated with asphaltic cutback oil to protect them from wear and to make plastic bags less slippery.

Machine gun and other bunkers were also built of soil-filled 55-gallon drums. Since drums set side-by-side had weak points that were easily penetrated by gunfire, the front and preferably the interior had to be faced with sandbags or two layers of drums used. Sandbags offered protection from metal fragments when struck by gunfire. CONEX machine gun bunkers had a firing port cut into the end opposite the door and the CONEX emplaced at ground level or semi-sunk. It was then faced and roofed with sandbags and a firing port was made using 2in. × 10in. planks. Sometimes one of the doors would be removed and a smaller entry provided by sandbagging it in.

Mortar positions were usually circular (60mm – 6ft; 81mm – 8ft; 4.2in. – 12ft) but sometimes square, with an attached ammunition bunker. They too could be built above ground, semi-sunk, or below ground. The parapet was at least two layers of sandbags thick. Sometimes a parapet of packed earth was built and covered with a shelved layer of sandbags. Soil-filled drums and ammunition boxes also revetted mortar pits. If the sandbag parapet was concrete-capped so was the pit's inside face. This allowed a black band with white degree or mil marks to be painted around the inside and marked to indicate the directions for defense concentrations (DEFCON). Ammunition ready racks were sometimes emplaced in the sidewalls for DEFCON rounds, with pre-cut charges and illumination rounds with their time fuses pre-set. The floor remained earth to facilitate drainage.

Recoilless rifle positions were required to have an open rear and were ill suited to having a roof because of back blast over-pressure. A large area behind the rifle had to be kept clear of obstructions and debris, this being a triangular area about 100ft deep and 65ft wide for a 57mm recoilless rifle. The 106mm recoilless rifle was mounted on an M151A1C jeep. When issued with this weapon, A-teams were directed that it was to remain mounted on the jeep, which could not be used as a separate vehicle. This was frequently ignored and the weapon mounted as the team deemed necessary. Often several slightly elevated revetted positions were prepared around the perimeter to allow the rifle to be moved. Camps had mostly been constructed before they received a 106mm recoilless rifle, so sufficient space to accommodate its considerable back blast was scarce, thus restricting where they could be emplaced.

Occasionally, 16–20ft-high watchtowers and machine gun towers were built from logs, timbers, or steel framing. A popular type used a speed pallet as a floor with soil-filled 105mm howitzer ammunition boxes as protective walls. The boxes were held in place by steel frameworks made from barbed wire pickets. Such a tower inside the inner perimeter allowed a .50-cal. machine gun to be fired over other buildings into the outer barbed wire barriers. This was called a "Medal of Honor tower" as all one had to do to be awarded the Medal was climb the tower during an attack!

While manuals specified standard trench dimensions, in practice they varied greatly. They were commonly 2½ to 3ft across and comparatively shallow, but the depth depended on the type of parapet. Trench depth and parapet height together was usually at least chest-high. Parapets were robustly constructed and more permanent than merely piling up a soil parapet. They were usually made up of two layers of sandbags often capped with concrete. In the early or developing camps, piled earth parapets were sometimes used. These were usually thick, neat, well tamped, and often capped with a shelved layer of sandbags to prevent rain erosion. Another form was a shallow trench fronted by a 3ft-high, 2–3ft-wide soil-filled wall revetted on both sides by M8A1 planks or corrugated sheet metal, often with individual firing ports. Firing steps or slots were cut into the trench side at intervals with firing ports. In many instances firing steps had light overhead cover. Rather than having simple firing steps, some camps had 2–3-man bunkers for riflemen. Some perimeter trenches were built atop high earth berms. Perimeter trenches could be zigzag in form or built with right-angle turns. Zigzag communications trenches connecting different areas within the camp sometimes lacked parapets.

The perimeter berms were bulldozed into place by starting the bulldozer 300ft or more out and running in toward the perimeter, scraping a few inches off the surface to push it into a berm. This also had the effect of clearing the ground for the wire barriers. The bulldozer would then

It was common practice for USSF NCOs to give a crew of Strikers a few hours' head start filling sandbags. Then one or two NCOs would begin placing sandbags for a bunker as the Strikers raced to keep up the supply. All of them would expend mighty effort just to avoid the 20 push-ups the losers would have to knock out.

Construction costs were kept down by the use of local materials. These also substituted for standard materials that were frequently in short supply. Here a woodcutting crew delivers hardwood logs to be used for anti-sniper walls.

work the berm to dress it up, as would shovel-welding troops. Depending on the terrain and vegetation, the ground might be cleared another 300–1,000ft further out from the outer wire belt.

Sandbags were to be stacked with the runner (the edge without a seam) facing outward and seams facing inward, as were the chokes (the opening in each bag). Ideally they would be stacked with wet soil fill and pounded into a squared, brick-like shape with pieces of 4in. × 4in. lumber wielded by Strikers. Besides giving a neat appearance, this provided a more solid structure when the filler dried. American troops tended not to bother with this professional touch.

All weapon positions were provided with storage space for a considerable amount of ammunition. In the early days of the war it was quickly learned that once an attack commenced, ammunition resupply from central bunkers was virtually impossible. Weapon positions had to hold sufficient ammunition and additional stocks were sometimes stored nearby. Crew-served weapon positions were usually provided with a supply of small arms ammunition, grenades, and water. Even rations and LAWs were stocked in some.

Camps generally had a rundown and shabby appearance mixed with new construction. There were always new defenses and facilities under construction, being replaced or rebuilt, or repaired. Spoil from excavations, stacked construction materials, and debris from torn-down structures was apparent. Aerial photos of a given camp taken a few months apart revealed drastic changes, while photos of a camp taken a year or so apart were almost unreconcilable. The style in which structures were built could vary. For example, in the author's camp the three 81mm mortar pits were each of entirely different design, being built or rebuilt at different times under the supervision of different weapons NCOs.

Some wood-frame and corrugated metal buildings, especially in the inner perimeter, were painted, usually green. Metal roofs were seldom painted, as per most other buildings. The camp name was usually painted in large block letters atop the LLDB team house, usually in yellow, as this was more visible at night. The USSF's team number may have been painted atop their team house. A number was painted atop different main buildings in remote settings to enable the crews of supporting aircraft to identify them. A Vietnamese flag flew in the inner perimeter. The US flag could not be flown; these were Vietnamese bases. The US flag usually adorned the wall inside the USSF team house.

Camp defense

Camps could be overrun if the enemy was determined enough, possessed the strength and firepower, was able to obtain good intelligence, and was willing to pay the price in casualties. Even if a camp was completely overrun the VC/NVA usually suffered more casualties than the defenders.

The defenders

A Camp Strike Force (CSF) was a battalion-size unit consisting of three or four rifle companies, one or two combat reconnaissance platoons (CRP), and a political warfare team. Actual strength varied greatly, from 250–550, with the average somewhere in between. The troops at a particular camp could be of a single ethnic group or from two or three different groups. For example, in I and II CTZ they were mostly Montagnard; in III and IV CTZ they were Cambodian (born and raised in Vietnam) and Vietnamese, though some Montagnard Strikers were found in III CTZ. Companies comprised troops from a single ethnic group.

A CSF company consisted of some 130–150 troops organized into a headquarters, a weapons platoon and three rifle platoons with three ten-man squads. The weapons platoon had two machine guns and two 60mm mortars. Often it was not organized as such, with the machine guns assigned to rifle platoons and the mortars retained in the camp. The CRP (a second one was authorized in late 1969) could conduct both reconnaissance and small-scale combat operations either independently or while accompanying a company. The 16-man political warfare team provided civic action and morale services.

The USSF A-team was authorized 12–14 men, although they were typically understrength. The A-team officially served as advisors to the LLDB and the CSF, but in reality they oversaw combat operations and the operation of the camp. The similar-sized LLDB team officially commanded the camp and CSF, but often concerned themselves with the day-to-day running of the camp. In some camps, especially in the early days and when there was a threat of infiltration of the CSF by VC, a 20–60-man detachment of Nungs was provided as bodyguards for the A-team, under whose direct command they served. Nungs were ethnic Chinese who had fled North Vietnam after the communist takeover. They were fierce fighters and completely loyal to the Americans.

This observation post, atop one of the inner perimeter buildings, has a parapet built of soil-filled 105mm ammunition boxes. They are held in place by wood framing.

Life in a camp was not unduly harsh and could even be described as relaxed if enemy activity was light. Typically one company conducted a five-day combat operation, one or two others undertook training and external camp security, and another provided camp support on a rotational basis. Camp support included work details building, repairing, and maintaining bunkers, other structures and the wire; filling water trailers and distributing them about the camp, latrine burnout, trash collection and burning, grass cutting in the wire, checking the runway for debris, general

ABOVE LEFT The wood-frame building is protected from mortar fragments and sniper fire by soil-filled steel 8in. howitzer propellant charge tubes.

ABOVE RIGHT One loop of detonating cord is placed around the inside lip of a 155mm propellant tube and tamped with mud. This cuts out the bottom end, allowing the tubes to be welded together end-to-end for a drainage pipe.

camp clear-up, cleaning crew-served weapons, unloading aircraft delivering supplies, cleaning out drainage ditches, etc.

Strikers would escort Medical-Civic Action Program (MEDCAP) teams comprising USSF, LLDB, and political warfare team members visiting local villages. This was an essential activity as it assisted the locals, won support for the South Vietnamese government, kept the villagers on friendly terms, and provided an opportunity to gather information from villagers.

Children attended the camp school, USSF and LLDB medics treated dependents and villagers in the dispensary (from minor illnesses to delivering

Concrete footings and plumbing have already been installed for this below-ground dispensary. Locally hired laborers dump rock fill before the concrete slab is poured.

babies), dependents visited the local village market, family disputes were settled, and life went on. There were few distractions. Volleyball and soccer were the main sports. Card playing, a few television sets, and outdoor movies two to four times a week filled the evenings.

There was no standard allocation of crew-served weapons for a strike camp. Equipment authorization tables allocated weapons on the basis of avenues of approach. For mortars and recoilless rifles the tables authorized one per main avenue of approach, and one machine gun was authorized for each main and secondary avenue of approach. This led to a broad interpretation based on the A-team's assessment of approaches. Most camps could be attacked from any direction and unless one side of a camp was edged by a wide, deep river, the distribution of crew-served weapons generally had to cover a 360-degree perimeter. Camps built on rugged terrain in the mountains might allocate additional weapons to cover nearby draws and ravines from which an attack might be launched. Some weapons would be assigned to fire on hills, ridges, and wooded areas on which the attacker's supporting weapons might be positioned.

The shape and size of the camp had much to do with the numbers of crew-served weapons, especially machine guns on the perimeter. One to three .30-cal. M1919A6 machine guns were mounted in corner bunkers; especially if the camp's design had "sharp" pointed corners as on triangular or five-pointed star-shaped designs. Such corner bunkers had to cover the two sidewalls and a direct approach to the corner. Corner bunkers were key targets as they covered two walls as well as any attack aimed at the corner itself. For this reason they were larger and more heavily constructed than other perimeter bunkers. With six- and eight-sided camps, the corner bunkers were usually the same as the wall bunkers and had only one or two machine guns. Wall bunkers were equally spaced with one or two per wall, more if the camp was large or the bunkers were on the long sides of rectangular-shaped camps.

Sometimes .50-cal. M2 machine guns were mounted in key outer perimeter bunkers (usually centered on a wall), or atop inner perimeter bunkers or towers to allow them to fire over buildings in the outer perimeter and into the wire. Camps might possess one to four .50-cal. machine guns; they could be mounted on an M3 tripod or M31 pedestal mount. (The story that it is illegal to fire .50-cal. machine guns at personnel, but that it is permitted to "fire at their equipment," is a myth. There is no such restriction in the Hague or Geneva Conventions.)

One to four 57mm M18A1 recoilless rifles were provided and perhaps a single 106mm M40A1. Some camps, however, had no recoilless rifles. These weapons could be mounted on the outer perimeter to cover the main approaches or dominating terrain features, or atop inner perimeter bunkers to

Strike Force Weapons

In the early days, the CIDG was issued with a variety of obsolescent and foreign weapons:
- .30-cal. M1903A3 rifle (Springfield)
- .30-cal. M1 rifle (Garand)
- .30-cal. M1 and M2 carbines
- .30-cal. M1918A2 Browning automatic rifle (BAR)
- .45-cal. M3A1 submachine gun ("grease gun")
- 9mm m/45b submachine gun (Swedish Carl Gustaf)
- 9mm M/50 submachine gun (Danish Madsen)
- .30-cal. M1919A6 light machine gun (Browning)
- M8 grenade launcher (for carbine)

The semi- and full-automatic M2 carbine was declared the standard CIDG shoulder weapon in 1962, along with the BAR; some M1 rifles were retained. The 40mm M79 grenade launcher and 7.62mm M60 machine gun began to be issued in 1967. The M1919A6 remained the main perimeter defense machine gun. In early 1969 the 5.56mm M16A1 rifle replaced the M2 carbine, M1 rifle, and BAR.

USSF officers examine the sealed 55-gallon drums attached to a floating barracks at Camp My An, IV CTZ. Floating buildings were provided with porches, which served as boat docks when the camp flooded. Travel between buildings was accomplished by using native dugouts, 16ft fiberglass assault boats, or simply swimming.

Camps generally had three or four 81mm mortar "pits," usually located within the inner perimeter. This helped ensure their protection and being deep within the camp their 230ft minimum range allowed them to fire into the outer wire barriers. In the event of an attack they were operated by USSF with the help of trained Strikers. The 81mm mortar (1) was a devastating weapon capable of delivering up to 30 rounds per minute for a short time. The HE round had a 130ft casualty radius. To fire a DEFCON the mortar would be oriented in the designated direction, a common DEFCON elevation set, the first round fired, the traversing hand turned once followed

by another round, another turn until 4–6 rounds were dropped, and then repeated to create a curtain of steel.

Sandbags (2) revet the below-ground interior sides in this instance. The revetment walls here are two sandbag layers thick, but could be considerably thicker. It is further strengthened by soil-filled 155mm howitzer propellant bag steel shipping tubes (3) partly buried in the ground. The ready rack (4) holds HE rounds with the charges cut for pre-planned DEFCONs and illumination rounds with the time-delay fuse pre-set and the charges cut. The end cap from a fiberboard ammunition tube protects the 81mm M29A1 mortar's muzzle. A

poncho or canvas trap normally protected the weapon, which was typically cleaned every other day. Several hundred HE (5) and illumination (6) rounds are stacked in the ammunition bunker (7) on pallets along with WP (8). Numerous models of ammunition were used. WP rounds were stowed vertically to prevent the gooey WP from settling on one side, which would throw the rounds off balance and off line when fired. One of the .50-cal. ammunition cans (9) holds cleaning gear and the other is for unused propellant bags (charges) "cut" (removed) from rounds. Canvas curtains would normally cover the bunker door and ready racks.

allow them to fire over buildings in the outer perimeter and into the wire. The 57mm was provided with canister rounds and the 106mm with flechette rounds for anti-personnel use. Both had high explosive shaped-charge (HEAT) rounds for anti-tank use and white phosphorus (WP) smoke for screening and anti-personnel fire. The 57mm had a high explosive (HE) round while the 106mm had a high explosive, plastic (HEP) round for both anti-personnel and anti-tank use. Both had an effective range of up to 6,560ft for area targets on dominating terrain features the enemy might occupy.

Mortars were critical to the defense of the camps and large numbers were used. Each CSF company had two 60mm M19 mortars, normally left in the camp. This automatically gave the camp six or eight mortars. Several additional M19s might be provided, giving a camp ten or more. Three or four 81mm M29A1 mortars were also provided to place a curtain of steel around a camp. The 60mm mortars were positioned at roughly equal intervals inside the outer

This newly constructed sandbag bunker at My An is built on an earth mound above flood level. The barbed wire pickets help retain the sandbags and will be reinforced with barbed wire strands, then concrete-capped.

ABOVE This log and earth bunker was typical in early camps when sandbags were in short supply. Split logs are used for firing ports, as dimensioned lumber was scarce. The guard hut, protected from snipers by sandbags and from the sun by a thatch or corrugated steel roof, was a standard fixture.

perimeter. While their 165ft minimum range allowed them to fire into the wire, they were often sited to fire into the wire on the opposite side of the camp, thus allowing them to make better use of their minimum range. A mortar firing into the wire on the side of the camp on which it was emplaced could not bring the rounds in close enough. Mortar pits on the side of the camp under attack might receive direct fire and be unable to operate while mortars on the opposite were not under fire and could operate. The 81mm mortars in the inner perimeter, with a minimum range of 230ft, could fire into the outer wire.

One to four 4.2in. M30 mortars might be available. Camps usually had only one or two M30s, but those without 105mm howitzers might have additional

A camp's USSF and LLDB officers inspect a recently completed concrete bunker. The roof is several layers of sandbags contained by a concrete wall, covered by corrugated sheet metal for waterproofing, and topped by a burster layer of concrete blocks and rubble.

"four-deuces." The M30 had a minimum range of 2,525ft. It was ill-suited for direct camp defense, as rounds fell well outside the wire. It was useful for firing on enemy supporting weapons positions, dominated terrain, and suspected enemy assembly areas, as well as firing illumination. The 81mm and 4.2in. mortars could also provide fire support to local security patrols operating within some 2–3 miles of the camp, respectively.

All three types of mortar were provided with HE, WP, and illumination rounds. One of the most valuable roles of mortars was illumination. Continuous illumination by parachute-suspended flares was invaluable to illuminate the wire and attackers.

A very small number of camps dug-in disabled tanks, either a US 90mm M48A3 or an ARVN 76mm M41A3.

Conduct of the defense

The defense of a strike camp was a multi-layered exercise that required numerous proactive measures if it was to be successful. Aggressive search-and-clear operations conducted by the CSF in its TAOR kept the enemy off balance. A camp conducting successful operations made itself a candidate for attack though, so maintaining good relations with nearby villages and establishing agents inside them provided early warning of any attack in the planning. Platoon-size daylight security patrols would be conducted out to roughly two-thirds of a mile from the camp as well as close in, on the lookout for signs of enemy preparations. While a camp buttoned up for the night, ambush patrols established on likely avenues of approach meant that it was not blind to the outside world.

To attack a camp required that VC Main Force or NVA units be brought into the area, and signs of this build-up were often detected. The VC might attempt to gain support from villagers and even direct propaganda at the Strikers. It was seldom the case that a camp was totally surprised by an attack. When it was evident that an attack was pending MIKE Force, ARVN, or US units were often brought in to secure dominating terrain and conduct offensive operations to thwart the enemy's plans.

Ground attacks were typically launched with a main attack and one or two supporting attacks, making it difficult to determine which was the main attack. The supporting attacks held the defenders in their sectors rather than allow them to be moved to meet the main attack. Supporting weapons were to the flanks of the attack or on high ground, enabling them

ABOVE LEFT This bunker is beyond the norm, but Cai Cai was a frequent target for attacks. It is built with double walls of concrete-filled cinder block with packed earth between the walls. It fought off two major assaults in 1965. This bunker is on the riverside corner (see page 22 Cai Cai photo). Note the sloped barbed wire apron to hamper demolition charge-wielding sappers. A Claymore mine can be seen wired to a U-shaped picket below the bunker's right corner.

ABOVE RIGHT A typical machine gun bunker being constructed around a CONEX at Camp My Phuoc Try, A-411, IV CTZ. It will be topped by sandbags and a revetted entry passage built. A rifle firing port can be seen in the side. A larger and lower machine gun port is in the front.

Crew-served Weapons

Weapon	Weight	Range
.30-cal. M1919A6 MG	32½ lbs	1,090 yds
.50-cal. M2 MG	126 lbs	2,000 yds
60mm M19 mortar	45.2 lbs	2,200 yds
81mm M29A1 mortar	132 lbs	3,990 yds
4.2in. M30 mortar	672 lbs	6,000 yds
57mm M18A1 RR	40.2 lbs	1,300 yds
106mm M40A1 RR	460 lbs	1,090 yds
105mm M101A1 howitzer	4,980 lbs	12,000 yds

Exterior view of a 57mm M18A1 recoilless rifle position atop a machine gun bunker.

The 57mm M18A1 recoilless rifle (1) was developed at the end of World War II, but was no longer in use by conventional US forces. It had an effective range of 1,400 yards for point targets when fired from the M1917A1 tripod using its M86F telescopic sight. It could also be fired from the shoulder or on a folding bipod and monopod from the ground. The M302A1 HE and M308A1 WP were slightly less potent than 60mm mortar rounds and the

M307A1 HEAT achieved extremely poor penetration against armor. It was valuable in that long-range point targets could be easily hit owing to its high degree of accuracy. Even more valuable was the T25E5 canister round (2). Filled with 154 or 176 stacked cylindrical steel slugs (1.8 lbs), this shotgun-type round was effective to 170 yards. At 25 yards it had a 9-yard spread.

A 57mm recoilless rifle was often mounted atop inner perimeter machine

gun bunkers (3), allowing them to fire over outer perimeter buildings and into the wire. This position is atop a machine gun bunker built around a steel CONEX container (4). A pair of 3ft-diameter CMP halves filled with sandbags provides the firing platform. The weapon's considerable back blast required an open rear. A ready rack (5) holds HE and canister rounds. Additional ammunition is stowed inside the machine gun bunker.

Fire Arrow

A fire arrow was positioned on a pivoting mount near the center of a camp and usually shielded by a wall or fence to conceal it from enemy view. When a camp was attacked at night and supporting aircraft arrived on-station, the arrow was pointed in the direction of the main attack. All of the fuel-filled cans on the arrowhead were lit and then the number of cans on the arrow shaft, indicating the distance from the camp's perimeter to the enemy. Each lit can represented 330ft distance.

An 8–12ft arrow-shaped wooden steel barbed wire picket frame had one-gallon (No. 10) cans fastened to the broad arrowhead in a V-pattern and in a single line down the arrow's shaft. The cans were half-filled with sand and gasoline was poured in before use. The fire arrow was covered with a trap when not in use.

to engage targets on the perimeter and inside the camp. Intense mortar barrages usually preceded attacks. Sappers, though, were already in the wire, cutting lanes and deactivating Claymore mines and trip flares. Some may have penetrated the camp's interior to attack the TOC/commo bunker, team houses, generators, mortar positions, etc. This was seldom successful, but VC sympathizers in the Strike Force were sometimes more effective.

When an attack was suspected the perimeter guard was increased and a heightened state of alert maintained. When the attack was initiated or detected by sentries virtually all perimeter weapons opened fire, even if no movement was detected in their sectors. This was in case supporting attacks or infiltrators were elsewhere in the wire. Designated mortars began firing illumination all around the perimeter. As soon as the location of the attacks was determined the mortar defensive concentrations (DEFCON) were fired into the wire. The 105mm howitzers and 4.2in. mortars would open fire on pre-planned targets such as possible assembly areas and supporting weapon positions. Squads or platoons from other companies were sometimes dispatched from sectors not under attack to reinforce the endangered sector. Strength was not reduced to the point that other sectors were undermanned, in case other attacks developed.

The first hour or so was utter confusion. No matter how well a camp prepared, its defense could still be confused and disorganized, as is any combat action. Often a flare ship, a modified C-47 transport, arrived on-station and

USSF and LLDB weapons NCOs check a .30-cal. M1919A6 machine gun position at an outlying outpost. The hastily constructed position is made from a half-section of 4ft-diameter corrugated metal pipe and covered with plastic sandbags.

ABOVE LEFT A USSF NCO watches WP bursts from his camp's 4.2in. mortar. The entire trench and bunker complex is completely concrete-capped. Barbed wire pickets hold the corrugated trench revetting in place and are reinforced by plank spreaders jammed between them.

ABOVE RIGHT A USSF weapons NCO plots DEFCON sight elevation data on a mortar pit's firing data board. On the ground is an 81mm M374 HE round. Most of the charge bags on the fins will be removed because of the DEFCON's short range.

began dropping illumination, partly relieving mortars of that necessity. If the camp was within artillery range of other camps or firebases, and most were, pre-coordinated DEFCONs would be fired. Because of the moderate accuracy of artillery, these were plotted outside the wire and on possible assembly areas and nearby hills. The A-team would adjust artillery fire closer in once the situation stabilized.

RIGHT This is an example of a very early camp's 81mm mortar pit: merely a pit dug in the ground with a low sandbag parapet. The hooch behind it is constructed of thatch and bamboo rattan; typical local materials.

If the perimeter was penetrated, close-range fights among the buildings ensued, with even mortars being fired into the overrun area. Troops would be moved into the lateral communication trenches and took position in adjacent buildings in an effort to contain the penetration. This became extremely confused, as it was very difficult to coordinate the positioning of troops, conduct counterattacks, control panicked dependents, and determine exactly where the enemy was. Enemy individuals and small groups could easily spread through the camp amidst the darkness, confusion, and fires. Even if most of a camp was overrun, the inner perimeter and other pockets often held out until relief arrived or the attackers withdrew before first light.

If an attack did not overrun a camp within an hour or two, it usually failed. However, some successful attacks developed into all-night battles. At first light, close air support aircraft and attack helicopters arrived. Their support was critical, but as with artillery they could deliver their ordnance only so close to the camp.

ABOVE More elaborate 81mm mortar pits are seen here. These have broad earth parapets covered with stepped sandbags to prevent erosion. An ammunition bunker is incorporated into the wide parapets.

BELOW A seldom-issued 75mm M20 recoilless rifle is mounted in a concrete-capped firing position. Judging by the perspective of the background this position is mounted atop another bunker to allow it to fire into the outer barrier – a common practice when mounting a recoilless rifle.

A 57mm M18A1 recoilless rifle is inspected. It is mounted on an M1917A1 tripod, originally designed for the Browning water-cooled machine gun. This position has a low sandbag parapet.

Because of the artillery and air superiority the attackers would "hug" the camp's defenses, that is, get in as close as possible, penetrate into the camp, and intermingle to negate the heavy defensive firepower.

An overrun camp degenerated into a state of pandemonium and mass confusion. At some point the Strikers might break and run; others would continue to fight. Panic among the hundreds of dependents caused more problems, especially since the VC/NVA would shoot indiscriminately. While they sought to take American prisoners, they considered the CIDG traitors and seldom took prisoners. They executed the LLDB and their families.

Relief forces would be dispatched at first light as well. Unfortunately this did not always work because political conflicts, excessive caution, interservice rivalries, differing agendas, and poor coordination sometimes delayed or even prevented relief from being sent. All too often, relief forces were not dispatched for fear of heading into an ambush. For this and other reasons, Special Forces established MIKE Forces, their task being to provide reliable reaction forces under its own control. This, however, was of no consequence for camps that were overrun quickly.

Most relief forces were delivered by helicopter onto landing zones some distance from the camp. They had to fight their way into the camp, attack the attackers outside the camp, and seize dominating terrain around the camp. If the camp had been overrun, relief forces seldom found any live enemy; they had withdrawn into the mountains or jungle, taking as many of their dead as possible. The enemy would also recover weapons and munitions from the camp; surprisingly, they often left much behind. Their main goals in mounting an attack were to destroy a camp that had been causing them difficulties, demonstrate their superiority to local villages, and achieve a political and psychological victory.

Strikers wheel a 105mm M101A1 howitzer into a newly completed firing position revetted by vertical stakes and sandbags. One or two ammunition bunkers were attached to each "gun pit."

The test of battle

Scores of camps, in fact most, were attacked at one time or another, but only seven camps actually fell. Attacks ranged from simple harassment while the camps were under construction to major assaults and sieges. Some camps were all but overrun before counterattacks or reinforcements drove out the attackers. No two battles were the same and only examples can be given. These examples describe a camp which almost fell, but held out, a completely successful defense, and a camp which fell to overwhelming odds.

The first CIDG camp to be overrun was Hiep Hoa on the Plain of Reeds northwest of Saigon, in the early morning hours of November 24, 1963. The camp was poorly prepared to repel an attack, morale was low, and VC who had infiltrated the CSF contributed to its downfall. Of the five USSF in the camp, four were captured.

Attack on Nam Dong

The Camp Nam Dong attack is an example of a vicious close-quarters battle to prevent a camp from being completely overrun. The camp, in the northern portion of I CTZ in a remote area, was located at the intersection of two valleys used by the VC as infiltration routes, some 15 miles from Laos. It was also responsible for protecting nine Montagnard villages and their 5,000 inhabitants, but it had been decided to turn the camp over to the Vietnamese and convert it to Civil Guard use (predecessor of the Regional Forces) because of the area's poor recruiting potential. The three CIDG companies each numbered 80-plus men rather than 154. Two companies were Montagnard and one Vietnamese.

The situation at Nam Dong was perilous. The camp was situated on less-than-desirable defensive terrain, the Vietnamese district chief was uncooperative, relations with the LLDB were strained, and there were fights between the Vietnamese company and the USSF team's Chinese Nung bodyguards. This

Nam Dong Standoff. Members of A-726 fight off the attackers from an 81mm mortar position in the early morning of July 6, 1964. (Frank M. Thomas ®)

RIGHT **Attack on Camp Nam Dong, 02.26 hours, July 6, 1964.**

Key:
1. Main VC attack.
2. Secondary VC attacks.
3. VC supporting fire.

A. USSF team house (command post, operations center, USSF quarters, civilian employee quarters).
B. Nung quarters, supply room, communications room.
C. LLDB team house (camp HQ, LLDB quarters).
D. Dispensary.

E. Nung quarters.
F. Communications bunker.
G. USSF mess hall.
H. Helicopter pad.
I. TOC pit ("swimming pool") and spoil pile.
J. Stacked concrete blocks (for TOC).
K. Fire arrow.
L. 81mm M1 mortar position (×3).
M. 60mm M2 mortar position (×2).
N. Nung mess hall.
O. Ammunition bunker (×3).

P. .30-cal. M1919A6 machine gun bunker (x3).
Q. Gate.
R. Entry road.
S. Outer wire barrier.
T. Outer perimeter trench.
U. Communications trench.
V. Inner perimeter wire barrier.

Unlettered buildings around the outer perimeter are Striker barracks. The view of the camp is looking towards the north.

degenerated into a shootout between the Nungs and Vietnamese the day before the attack, but the Americans put a halt to it before there were casualties. Some 100 miles to the south, undermanned Camp Polei Krong in II CTZ had been overrun on July 4, 1964. Seven USSF were wounded in the attack, but all SF personnel escaped. Unfortunately the USSF at Nam Dong had not been informed of Polei Krong's fall, which occurred two days before the attack on their camp.

Detachment A-726, detached from the 7th SFGA in the United States, arrived for a six-month tour at the end of May to relieve the in-place team. A-726 would continue making improvements to the camp, turn it over to the Civil Guard, then establish a new camp closer to the border at Ta Co. As soon as the new team arrived the VC increased its propaganda effort and harassment of local villages. In the days before the attack, patrols reported the villagers to be nervous and refusing to provide information. About 20 VC sympathizers were suspected in the Vietnamese company. These unstable conditions were exacerbated by the fact that almost 300 surplus weapons were in the camp awaiting shipment out, making an attack on the camp all the more desirable to the VC.

The 12-man USSF team with an attached Australian Special Air Service advisor, 60 Nungs, seven LLDB, and 381 Strikers defended the camp. CIDG dependents lived in Nam Dong Village a few hundred yards to the northeast. A Seabee-built north-south gravel airstrip was situated a couple of hundred yards to the east, and a small river flowed parallel with the airfield about 550 yards further east. A small outpost was located 165 yards to the south-southeast on a ridge. Forested low ridges several hundred yards away surrounded the camp. Further off, mountains rose over the camp.

The camp was a freeform, roughly oval shape, as was common for early camps, and measured about 820ft × 1,150ft. The perimeter trench relied on firing steps with a few open machine gun positions. There were machine gun bunkers at the main gate and in the southeast and southwest corners. The only barrier was a 4ft-high five-strand barbed wire fence with *punji* stakes. Because of the camp's scheduled conversion, grass had been allowed to grow high in the wire. Striker barracks were positioned around the perimeter. The entry road ran north from the northeast corner, with a gate in both the outer and inner wire barriers. The gates, wood-frame with interwoven barbed wire, were kept locked at night and were not opened under any circumstances. A man-sized gate beside the main gate allowed access to the inner perimeter. It could only be opened at night with an American present and covered by a Nung. A helicopter pad was located on the west side of the road just outside the outer perimeter.

The inner perimeter was larger than usual: 260ft × 395ft, oval, and surrounded by a similar wire fence only 100–130ft inside the outer perimeter.

Company 121

Company 122

Company 123

49

There was no perimeter berm or trench. The inner buildings were partly protected by 3ft-thick, 4ft-high log crib anti-sniper walls. The buildings themselves were built in the local Montagnard-style with thatch roofs and rattan walls. Besides several small buildings, there were 24ft × 60ft and 24ft × 40ft longhouses containing the USSF team house and other facilities. Some references suggest that the inner perimeter was built around a former French outpost, but this was not the case. On the inner perimeter's east side was a large pit, known as the "swimming pool," the future TOC, and a 7ft-high mound of earth and rocks plus three stacks of concrete blocks.

On the east side, but outside the inner perimeter's wire, were three sandbag ammunition bunkers enclosed in their own wire. Inside the inner perimeter were three 81mm and two 60mm mortar pits manned by USSF and Nungs. The mortar pits were semi-sunk with the below-ground sides revetted with smooth rounded rocks and low sandbag parapets. Each mortar pit had 350 rounds with more in the main ammunition bunkers. Some of the pits had recently had concrete ammunition bunkers added. The mortar pits were to become individual strong points that held out through the assault. A single 57mm recoilless rifle was to be carried by the team sergeant to where it was needed. The strike companies each had only one 60mm handheld mortar with 12 rounds, and two machine guns.

The USSF and Nungs were on full alert on the morning of the attack, July 6. The Strikers were lackadaisical, with most turning in. Years later it was found that some 100 Strikers were VC with orders to slit the throats of those sleeping nearby, remove their own uniforms, and join the assault wearing loincloths as did other attackers. The 800–900-man assault force – two VC Main Force battalions (these units were never identified) – positioned one 81mm and three 60mm mortars, a 57mm recoilless rifle, and machine guns on ridges to the north, northwest, and southwest of the camp. The six-man outpost outside the camp had their throats cut in their sleep.

The first mortar rounds impacted at 02.26 hours, hitting the USSF mess hall and team house and setting them on fire. Rounds were landing continuously and grenades were being thrown from the wire. The Americans at first thought another fight had broken out between the Nungs and Vietnamese. The team communications NCO immediately alerted the B-team by radio and called for a flare ship, but it was unable to take off because the airfield from which it operated had no runway lights. The communications room was hit as the commo man darted out and soon the supply room and most of the inner perimeter buildings were ablaze. Camp Nam Dong now had no means of communication with the outside world.

Americans and Nungs were manning the mortar pits while other Nungs were firing from the inner perimeter. Some VC sappers were shot inside the inner perimeter. Mortar and 57mm rounds were landing inside the inner perimeter and most of the Americans were soon wounded. The Australian SAS warrant officer was killed. To make matters worse, the US 57mm recoilless rifle proved to be defective. (From the description of the 57mm's loading problem, the author believes the fiberboard canister rounds may have swollen in the humidity, preventing them from being chambered.)

A demolition team was killed attempting to blow the main gate. Small infiltration attacks came from the south, southeast, west, and north, but the main attack struck from the southeast. Over 100 VC attacked in waves, their progress being halted by three Americans and a few Nungs whose efforts ensured that none of the attackers made it over the fence. On the east side, CSF Company 122 was completely overrun. The assistant communications NCO was killed fighting off VC who had penetrated near the "swimming pool."

The American and Nung defense was centered on their mortar pits, continuously firing two HE, then two WP, then one illumination round. Individual VC and sympathizers were making it through from all directions and being shot at the edge of the pits. The defenders of the 60mm mortar pit by the main gate were forced to withdraw under a continuous barrage of grenades, their team sergeant having been killed and the team commander left for dead. In fact the team commander regained consciousness and vacated the mortar pit, taking the mortar with him. Despite having been wounded several times, he set up the mortar behind a stack of blocks and directed a group of wounded Nungs to fire it while he continued to rally other defenders. The fight continued at close range, but the mortar positions were now down to less than a dozen rounds.

By 06.00 hours the VC fire was dwindling and the flare ship finally arrived, allowing the mortars to concentrate on firing HE. The VC began withdrawing and a transport airdropped ammunition, radios, batteries, and medical supplies by parachute to the defenders. Pre-packaged emergency resupply bundles were kept on hand by B-teams for such contingencies. VC snipers and rear guards continued to harass the smoldering camp as the main body withdrew to Laos. A Civil Guard company arrived at 08.00 hours, having been ambushed twice en route. Two hours later, a 100-man relief force of USSF and CIDG arrived in US Marine Corps helicopters from the B-team.

Two USSF and the Australian SAS warrant officer were dead and seven Americans wounded. The Strike Force lost 55 dead and 65 wounded; many others had fled or joined with the VC. The LLDB had done little if anything to defend the camp, adding weight to the belief that the LLDB commander was in league with the VC. The bodies of 62 VC attackers were left behind, but as many as three times that number were believed killed and a large number of others wounded. Virtually every building in the camp was burned and the VC managed to make off with over 13,000 carbine rounds from one of the ammunition bunkers. A crater analysis team counted approximately 1,000 mortar craters.

The two dead Americans were each awarded the Distinguished Service Cross, the second highest American award. The other team members received Silver and Bronze Stars. Capt. Roger H. C. Donlon, commanding A-726 became the first soldier to be awarded the Medal of Honor in Vietnam. Detachment A-224, arrived from Camp An Diem, which was closed, replaced A-726 and completely rebuilt Camp Nam Dong in a triangular shape prior to turning it over to the Civil Guard in September 1964. The reconstituted A-726, with five original members, opened Camp Ta Co in September 1964 as planned.

Camp Nam Dong had held out despite its poor defenses, the large number of turncoats, and the poor performance of the remaining Strikers and LLDB. It held because of the vigilance and loyalty of the Nungs, a strong centralized inner perimeter capable of holding out when the rest of the camp was overrun, sufficient ammunition stowed in the mortar positions, and the resoluteness and cohesion of the USSF team.

Battle for Loc Ninh

Located in the northern part of III CTZ eight miles from the Cambodian border and on the east edge of War Zone C, a largely VC-controlled area, Camp Loc Ninh experienced repeated attacks over several days, and defending against them involved conventional US forces.

In late 1967 the camp became a focus of VC attacks as part of a larger campaign, the timing of the attacks coinciding with the inauguration of President Nguyen Van Thieu. Provincial Route 13 ("Thunder Road") was the main road through the area and led to Saigon 62 miles to the south. Loc Ninh District Town ("district" equates to a US county) was one mile northeast of the camp. Regional Force and Popular Force units secured the town from the Loc Ninh Subsector compound. Some 650 yards to the west was a village for rubber-plantation workers. Civilians in the area were mostly pro-government.

An earlier camp had been opened 650 yards southeast of the new site in September 1962. The new Camp Loc Ninh was established in December 1966 by

Camp Plei Me, A-255, II CTZ endured a grueling siege from October 19–27, 1965 requiring reinforcement by Project Delta and MIKE Force troops. The commitment of US troops to the battle saw their first major combat in Vietnam. The camp is a classic triangular shape, but with the inner perimeter abutting the right wall. Both perimeters consist of zigzag trenches with firing port-pierced parapets. Note the corner machine gun bunkers extending beyond the perimeter and backed by a large fighting bunker. In the center of the inner perimeter is the heavily sandbagged TOC.

A-331 for border surveillance. Route 13, which continued on into Cambodia, for all practical purposes ended at Loc Ninh. No effort was made to secure the neglected road beyond the town, but US and ARVN units kept the road open, during daylight, all the way to Saigon. A-331 was under the command of Capt. Florencio Berumen.

The camp was unusually, but efficiently shaped. It was an elongated diamond shape oriented from southwest to northeast, but its four sides were indented with shallow "Vs," in effect giving it eight walls. The perimeter was a high berm topped with a zigzag trench and two-man fighting positions. These were constructed of sandbags with a speed pallet roof topped by one or two layers of sandbags. A firing port was provided in the front. The trench was unrevetted with a one-layer-thick sandbag parapet. Several coils of razor concertina wire fronted the berm. At the inner point of the indented "Vs" was a machine gun bunker with others on the corners. The southwest end was blunt and had two machine gun bunkers several yards apart.

The entrance road ran from the airfield, which ran from southeast to northwest just outside the wire, curving through the wire barriers to enter the camp at the southeast wall's "V." Any attacker attempting to use the road would be exposed to short-range flanking fire from their right for the entire length of the wall. Above-ground Striker barracks were spotted at irregular intervals around the perimeter. A total of 530 Cambodians, Vietnamese, Montagnards, and Nungs manned four companies and a CRP. One company was assigned to each of the four walls.

The inner perimeter was six-sided and surrounded by a concertina wire-fronted low berm. There were machine gun or fighting bunkers at each corner, but no trench line. The inner berm was revetted on the inside and served only as a wall from which to fire from behind, but with no rear protection. Six wood-frame, corrugated metal-roofed buildings were inside the inner perimeter, each

RIGHT **Battle for Loc Ninh, October 29 to November 3, 1967.**

Key:

A. USSF team house.
B. Communications bunker.
C. USSF quarters.
D. Supply room.
E. LLDB team house and quarters.
F. 81mm M29 mortar positions.
G. .30-cal. M1919A6 machine gun bunkers (x 9).
H. Gate.
I. Outer perimeter berm with trench and fighting positions.

J. Inner wire barrier.
K. Outer wire barrier.
L. Entry road.
M. Airfield.
N. Turnaround pad.
O. Fire support base.
P. Loc Ninh District Town.

1. VC attack Loc Ninh District Town, 01.15 hours, October 29.
2. VC attack Camp Loc Ninh, 01.20, October 29.

3. Two CIDG companies relieve Loc Ninh District Town, October 29.
4. 2d Battalion, 28th Infantry airmobiles in and establishes firebase, 06.30 hours, October 29.
5. VC attack Loc Ninh District Town, 00.55 hours, October 31.
6. VC attack Camp Loc Ninh, 00.55 hours, October 31.
7. VC attack Camp Loc Ninh, 00.50 hours, November 2.

running parallel to a wall. Most were connected by covered walkways. Most of the 60mm and 81mm mortar pits were built above ground with vertical sandbag parapets. A hastily built second trapezoid-shaped stronghold was located in the northeast arm of the diamond with a low berm, mortar positions, and CIDG quarters.

The camp was built in a rubber plantation and as few of the trees as possible were cut down in order to preserve them for cultivation. For this reason the cleared area around the camp was 100 yards or less in width. The plantation was devoid of underbrush and the trees were planted in neat rows, providing good visibility. Two wire barriers surrounded the camp with tanglefoot strung between them. On the airfield side the barriers were light, consisting of 6ft-high seven-strand barbed wire on U-shaped pickets with two stacked coils of concertina. On the sides facing the rubber plantation it was considerably denser, the inner belt consisting of three back-to-back coils of concertina stacked two-high with an additional coil atop the third inner row. The outer belt was a large diamond while the inner belt followed the outline of the outer berm about 100ft out, beyond hand grenade range.

The enemy began preparations for the battle in early October 1967 when the headquarters of the 9th VC Division located itself north of Loc Ninh. The division's 272d and 273d VC Regiments were positioned near the Cambodian border to the north and the 271st to the south. The latter was driven out of the area by engagements with the 1st US Infantry Division in late October, suffering heavy losses in the process, and would not participate in the forthcoming battle. The 165th VC Regiment, which had participated in an almost successful August attack on Camp Tong Le Chon to the southeast, provided one or two battalions to reinforce the remaining regiments. These were all-VC Main Force units heavily augmented by NVA. They were well-armed light infantry units, not guerrillas. Each of the battalions had a strength of 300–400 men. The 84A NVA Artillery Regiment, equipped with 122mm rockets and 120mm mortars, supported the attack. Numerous 12.7mm anti-aircraft machine guns were employed and the assault force had Soviet-made flamethrowers.

US intelligence was aware of these enemy movements and an attack on Loc Ninh was expected, but not of the ferocity and the tenacity actually experienced. The 1st Infantry Division's plan was to airmobile in four US battalions and position them in a box around Loc Ninh, leaving the attackers trapped within. Prior to the attack, one Loc Ninh company was patrolling five miles north of the camp. The Strikers in the camp were fully alert and all positions were manned.

The VC objective was to seize both the camp and the town. To this end the 272d Regiment approached from the northeast and the 273d from the west on the night of October 28. The attack was launched at 01.15 hours on October 29 when mortars were fired at the subsector compound northeast of the camp. The first mortar rounds struck Loc Ninh minutes later as a 273d Regiment battalion attacked from the west. VC sappers managed to penetrate the subsector compound. Flare ships and AC-47D "Spooky" gunships were quickly dispatched. Mortar fire on the camp (82mm and 120mm) was heavy until 02.50 hours, then sporadic until it ceased altogether at 05.30 hours. The VC withdrew leaving 149 dead in the camp's wire. Few of the mortar rounds fired had actually landed inside the camp.

At dawn, two CIDG companies from the camp, led by USSF, moved into the town and cleared the subsector compound of VC, rescuing the US advisor and Vietnamese district chief holed up in the TOC. At 06.30 hours part of 2d Battalion, 28th Infantry and two artillery batteries airmobiled onto the Loc Ninh Airfield and established a firebase at the field's southwest end. Other American battalions were helicoptered into the area to begin establishing the "box," while additional units were positioned along possible VC withdrawal routes between Loc Ninh and the border. Throughout the day, American units made sporadic contact with the VC fighters.

At 00.55 hours on October 31, two battalions of the 272d Regiment struck the camp and subsector from the northeast and east, attacking the camp from across the airfield. An estimated 200 rounds of 82mm and 120mm mortar and 18 122mm rockets hit the camp along with RPGs and recoilless rifles. The assault was pinned down and devastated by coordinated fire from the camp, the firebase, close air support, and attack helicopters. Some American troops from the firebase reinforced the camp. The VC withdrew at 09.15 hours leaving 110 dead around the airfield. More American units were inserted around the area to block the withdrawing VC.

There was no attack in the morning of November 1 other than a few mortar rounds at 02.00 hours, believed to be covering fire while the VC recovered weapons and wounded from the wire. A final attack was launched at Loc Ninh at 00.50 hours on November 2, but this was easily repulsed as the VC were completely demoralized and seen to be dropping their weapons and fleeing after losing over 100 dead. American units in the area killed even more VC in a series of scattered contacts. Through it all, one CIDG company with two USSF remained in the field from October 28, ambushing VC patrols and calling in air strikes. Firefights and ambushes continued around Loc Ninh until November 7. In all, over 1,000 VC were killed and a great number of weapons, including many crew-served, were captured by CIDG and US troops.

The defense of Loc Ninh was extremely successful. The CIDG were well trained, motivated, and morale was high. Camp alert and defense plans were well developed and rehearsals had been conducted. Internal communications were excellent and remained intact throughout the assault. The radio tower was destroyed, but communications were immediately re-established using an underground antenna system. The camp was well built and the defenses were in good shape. The only weak point in the defenses was the light wire barriers on the airfield side. Too much reliance was placed on the breadth of the airfield acting as a hindrance to attack, when in fact the VC took a gamble and attempted to assault across the open to more easily penetrate the lighter wire. Nevertheless the massive firepower brought to bear from the camp, firebase, and air devastated them. The barrages of massed Claymore mines were particularly effective in breaking up their assaults. The camp easily withstood the heavy barrages of mortars, rockets, and direct-fire weapons, though the 122mm rockets and 120mm mortars did destroy some of the northeast berm's trench line. The major reason for the success of the defense was the close coordination and cooperation between USSF, LLDB, Vietnamese subsector, and US Army units. Loc Ninh's defenders suffered light casualties: four USSF slightly wounded, six CIDG dead, and 39 wounded.

Camp Loc Ninh was further developed and its defenses strengthened. In August 1968 an NVA attack was beaten back even though bad weather denied the defenders any air support. By 1969, when the author visited the camp, its perimeter trench parapets and upgraded machine gun bunkers were concrete-capped. The CSF was converted to the 74th Border Ranger Battalion in August 1970. In April 1972, during the opening of the NVA offensive to seize An Loc to the south, Loc Ninh, defended by ARVN infantry and border rangers, fell to the 5th VC Division after a four-day battle.

Fall of Lang Vei

Special Forces first came to the Khe Sanh valley in the extreme northwest corner of Vietnam in July 1962, when they established a camp north of Khe Sanh Village utilizing some former French pillboxes. Route 9 ran east-to-west through the valley from the coast and into Laos. When the Marines established a base at Khe Sanh Airfield in late December 1966, Detachment A-101 moved its border surveillance camp eight miles west and closer to the Laotian border,

The fall of Lang Vei, 00.50 hours, February 7, 1968.

This view of Lang Vei is looking south. Only the central position and the southeast portion of the camp are depicted; insert (i) shows the complete camp layout and unit positions. Some of the 11 attacking PT-76 tanks (in red outline) have penetrated the camp and are being engaged by tank-hunter teams armed with LAWs. Seven PT-76s were knocked out, two by the south 106mm recoilless rifle and five by LAWs. One of those destroyed by a LAW beside the TOC had its turret blown off. Four of those knocked out by LAWs were recovered by the NVA who left behind only the one hit beside the TOC and the two hit on the south approach by the 106mm recoilless rifle. The design of the underground command bunker is shown in inset (ii), depicting the steel drum-protected entrance and the above-ground OP bunker.

Key:

A. Underground tactical operations center with above-ground bunker and observation post.
B. Rock-filled drum strongpoint.
C. USSF team house.
D. Dispensary.
E. Emergency medical bunker.
F. Supply bunker.
G. Ammunition bunker (×2).
H. 4.2in. M30 mortar.
I. 81mm M29 mortars (x5).
J. 106mm M40A1 recoilless rifles.
K. 57mm M18A1 recoilless rifle.
L. Provincial Route 9.
M. Company 101
N. Company 102
O. Company 103
P. Company 104
Q. 1st CPP/3d CRP
R. 2d CRP

1. Main attack conducted by five PT-76 tanks, infantry battalion, and two sapper companies.
2. Secondary attack by four PT-76 tanks and infantry battalion.
3. Supporting attack by two PT-76 tanks and infantry battalion.

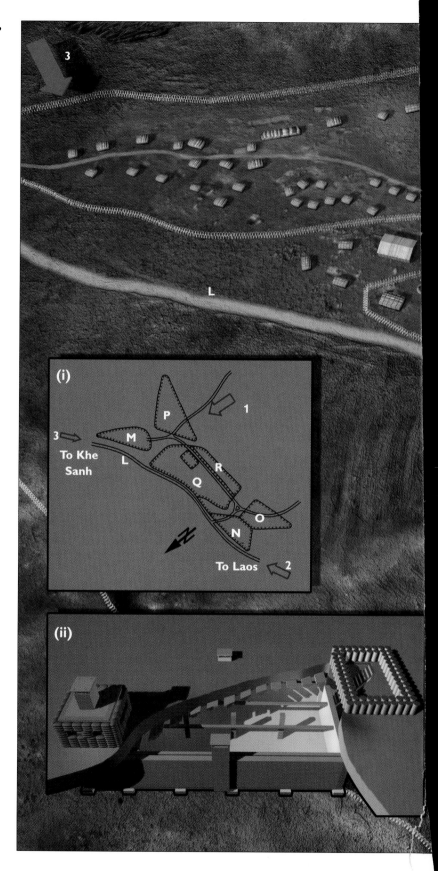

reopening on December 8 as Camp Lang Vei. The Hill Fights north of the Marines' Khe Sanh Combat Base raged throughout April and May 1967 as the NVA maneuvered in the area.

The camp, still unfinished, was attacked by a tank- and mortar-supported NVA company on May 4. The tanks did not penetrate the camp, but provided fire support. This harassing attack was repelled with the aid of Marine artillery from Khe Sanh. Two USSF were killed, including the A-team commander, and five wounded along with 17 dead, 35 wounded, and 38 missing (most likely deserters) in the two CIDG companies. Old Lang Vei lacked good fields of observation and fire, did not have a strong inner perimeter, and could hold only two companies.

The new A-team commander had just arrived in-country and had never seen another Special Forces camp. He had the authority to relocate the camp anywhere within its TAOR so long as it was capable of reinforcement and built as a fighting camp with an inner perimeter. With these requirements in mind, he selected a site 1½ miles further west on an east–west ridge that provided excellent fields of observation and fire. He was not aware of the earlier use of tanks.

The new camp was dog-bone-shaped and built along the south side of Route 9. Its design was unusual in that there was no inner perimeter as such, but rather an irregular rectangular central position with two separate triangular or four-sided compounds on either end. This appears to have been because of the new commander's interpretation of the inner perimeter concept as well as terrain considerations. Built by Seabees, several of the key facilities were underground concrete structures. During construction it was discovered that some 1,400 French and Japanese mines covered the area, all of which had to be removed. Work was completed on September 27, 1967 and the camp formally opened.

The central position held a combined team house, TOC, medical and supply bunkers, two ammunition bunkers, and other support facilities, mostly below ground. These were built with 8in.-thick reinforced concrete walls because of the artillery threat. The TOC's 9in.-thick interlocking roof sections were prefabricated and helicoptered in. They were to be supported by 12in. × 12in. joists, but these were not provided. Surrounding the TOC was its own concertina barrier. There was one 4.2in., five 81mm, and 16 60mm mortar pits, two .50-cal. machine guns, and two fixed 106mm recoilless rifle positions, one covering Route 9 to the east and the other the southern approach. It had been assessed that if the NVA used tanks they would only provide supporting fire and would not enter the camp itself. The NVA, it was felt, would not squander armor on the camp, but save it for an attack on Khe Sanh. As a consequence of this assessment only 20 rounds of HEAT ammunition were available for the 106mm recoilless rifles. The 57mm recoilless rifles were ineffective as anti-tank weapons and no anti-tank mines were available. One hundred LAWs were delivered on December 29.

The four CSF company positions on the ends of the dog-bone each held an 81mm mortar and a 57mm recoilless rifle. There were no perimeter trenches or berms. Defenses were multi-man, semi-sunk fighting and living bunkers at closely spaced intervals. These varied in size and design and were built of sandbags, timbers, and speed pallets. A double-stacked concertina wire barrier beyond grenade range surrounded each company position, including the central. A similar outer barrier surrounded the whole in an irregular rectangle. The intervening ground was bulldozed clean and scores of Claymore mines emplaced. There were forty-seven M1919A6 and two M60 machine guns plus 39 Browning automatic rifles available, an inordinately high number of automatic weapons. MIKE Force Company 12 with six USSF reinforced the camp on December 22.

The NVA occupied Khe Sanh Village on January 21, 1968, cutting off the ground reinforcement route from Khe Sanh Base. The Marines had committed two companies for reinforcement, but now they could only arrive by helicopter. That same day the siege of Khe Sanh commenced with four NVA divisions: 40,000 troops. Relations between USSF and the Marines were strained as the Marines did not understand the Special Forces mission, nor did they want to have to support the exposed camp.

On January 24 the NVA routed the 33d Royal Laotian Battalion (BV33) just over the border, using tanks in the process. Seven of the tanks were detected by aircraft and one was destroyed. BV33 fled and arrived at Lang Vei with 500 troops and 2,200 dependents and refugees. The USSF positioned them in Old Lang Vei and arranged for food and supplies to be delivered. Four USSF were placed there to aid them. Field grade USSF officers were rotated through the camp, as the BV33 commander would not take orders from a junior USSF officer. On January 25–26 additional USSF augmented A-101. On January 30 a USSF accompanying a Laotian patrol was captured by the NVA outside Khe Sanh Village. The next day a MIKE Force patrol engaged an NVA battalion outside Khe Sanh Village and killed 54 of the fighters. Patrols around the camp continued and the NVA occasionally registered mortar hits on it.

On February 6 Lt.Col. Daniel F. Schungel, commanding Company C, 5th SFGA, arrived to take his turn as the senior officer present. That evening, 50 rounds of 152mm fired from within Laos rocked the camp. There were now 24 USSF, 14 LLDB, 282 CSF, and 161 MIKE Force. The three Vietnamese and one Montagnard CSF companies were small, numbering fewer than 60 men. One Vietnamese and two Montagnard 20-man CRPs defended the central position. One MIKE Force platoon was placed in each company position except the southwest and a fourth in the central position. At night these platoons would rotate occupation of an outpost just to the northwest.

At 00.50 hours on February 7, the defenders discovered tanks in the wire and the assault commenced. The main attack was from the south into the central position by 3d Battalion, 1st Regiment, 325th NVA Division; two sapper companies, and 9th Company, 198th Tank Battalion. The 5th Battalion, 24th Regiment, 304th NVA Division and 3d Company, 198th Tank Battalion launched the secondary attack from the west along Route 9. The 4th Battalion, 24th NVA Regiment conducted a supporting attack from the northeast. A 152mm battalion of the 675th Artillery Regiment and the 7th Engineer Regiment provided support. Each tank company had eight PT-76s, but only 11 were committed with the rest held in reserve. The infantry battalions were greatly understrength and it is estimated that 400-plus troops participated in the assault. The 8th Battalion, 66th Regiment, 325th NVA Division attacked Old Lang Vei.

The first tank penetration was made in the southeast compound by four of the PT-76 amphibious tanks approaching from the south. The PT-76 was armed with a 76.2mm main gun and 7.62mm coaxial machine gun, had a 3–4-man crew, weighed in at 14 tons, and was protected by 11–14mm armor. A USSF NCO destroyed two of the tanks outside the wire with a 106mm recoilless rifle. Five more PT-76s came down Route 9 from the west and another two along Route 9 from the east. The USSF called Khe Sanh for artillery support, arguing with the

A burned-out PT-76 tank rests beside the collapsed Lang Vie underground TOC's roof. On the right-hand end is the concrete observation bunker. Its roof and observation cupola were collapsed and the exterior sandbag revetting blown from the walls by the force of satchel charges. On the left end is the rock-filled drum barricade protecting the entrance to the TOC.

A PT-76 tank memorialized at Lang Vei. The legend reads: "The cadre [crew] of this tank inspired the people to rise up and fight to victory." All that remains of the camp is some broken concrete walls that were part of a bunker. (Danny Wright, Australian Army Training Team, Vietnam, attached to II Corps MIKE Force)

Marines that they were indeed under tank attack. Air strikes were also called for. The USSF in the old camp with BV33 directed air strikes when aircraft arrived. The USSF command group organized anti-tank teams, but most of the LAWs either misfired or were duds. One PT-76 was destroyed and its crew shot as they exited, but others crushed defensive positions while sappers blasted bunkers with satchel charges and flamethrowers as the camp was overrun. Another PT-76 had its turret blown off when its ammunition exploded after a LAW hit it beside the TOC.

Seven of the USSF and some LLDB and CIDG were trapped in the TOC. The NVA made repeated attempts to flush them out with flamethrowers, satchel charges, and tear gas grenades, but they would not surrender. Some indigenous personnel surrendered and were executed after exiting. The Americans continued to hold out even after massive demolition charges blew in the bunker before dawn.

USSF and CIDG personnel were still holding out in other parts of the camp. The three USSF with BV33 convinced some of the Laotians to counterattack. The three continued to direct air strikes and led five counterattacks until two of them were killed. Some USSF and CIDG managed to exfiltrate from the overrun camp. The Marines would not send a relief force, but a USSF-led MACV-Studies and Observation Group (MACV-SOG) Command and Control North reaction force was helicoptered in from its FOB at Khe Sanh Combat Base. Some 20 SOG USSF and 30 Strikers were delivered to Old Lang Vei at 17.15 hours to aid in the recovery of survivors. Once the USSF survivors had been flown out, some of the recovery force had to fight their way back to Khe Sanh on foot. CIDG and Laotian survivors who made it to Khe Sanh were disarmed by the Marines and held in a secure area until identified as friendly by USSF.

Fourteen USSF made it out; only one was unwounded and a further ten were missing. Three of the ten were released from captivity in 1973 along with the one captured earlier. All of the others were verified killed or presumed dead. Of the CIDG, 117 of the CSF (29 wounded) were recovered and 127 of the MIKE Force (32 wounded). The CIDG were credited with resolutely defending the camp, at least half of those killed dying at their positions. Nine LLDB survived (three wounded). NVA losses were estimated at 250 dead and seven PT-76 tanks knocked out. All of the Americans involved in the defense were decorated. Sgt. 1st Class Eugene Ashley, Jr. was posthumously awarded the Medal of Honor for his repeated counterattacks from the old camp. The Marines awarded A-101 the Presidential Unit Citation. The presence of tanks and the possibility of their use in a direct assault had been underestimated.

Because of its exposed position, incomplete defenses, small defense force, and the presence of massive artillery-supported NVA forces, Lang Vei probably should have been abandoned earlier.

Tanks attacked only one other camp: Ben Het in CTZ II on March 3, 1969. Two of the ten PT-76s involved were knocked out by US Army M48A3s; the others withdrew. They were never used against Khe Sanh because of the presence of heavier Marine tanks, large numbers of 106mm recoilless rifles, and massed artillery and air support.

Aftermath

With the withdrawal of US forces from Vietnam the CIDG Program was terminated on December 31, 1970. The LLDB was dissolved the next day. Between May 1970 and January 1971, some 14,000 CIDG personnel with the LLDB were transferred to the ARVN and converted to Border Rangers. This new organization continued the former border interdiction mission from existing camps. Other CSFs were converted to Regional Forces (a local militia security force), a process begun in 1969. The 5th SFGA was gradually phased out and the Group colors left Vietnam on March 3, 1971.

Some camps in stable areas were closed in 1969. Most of the B- and C-team camps were closed at the end of 1970, though some were converted for use by Border Rangers. Most of the closed camps were turned over to US or ARVN forces, after many of the buildings had been dismantled and used to upgrade and repair other camps. Many of the old CSF camps, whether occupied by Border Rangers, Regional Forces, or ARVN troops, saw action in the remaining years of the war and played a part in the final battles as the NVA overran South Vietnam in 1975. Some of the old camps along the border with Cambodia subsequently remained in use by the new regime.

Regardless of their eventual fate, the CIDG camps had largely accomplished their goal. They had established a government presence in remote areas where it was impossible to keep conventional units on a permanent basis; protected villages from exploitation by the VC; interdicted and harassed enemy infiltration and activities in the border and other areas; and allowed US, ARVN, and other Free World Forces to operate in more critical areas. The CSFs were low-cost, economy-of-force units. It would have required another seven more costly ARVN divisions to occupy the remote areas if the CIDG Program had not been established.

At a unit cost of $20–30,000 the camps proved to be comparatively cheap to build and maintain, though the cost rose as newer camps were built more stoutly. Some have questioned the lack of standardization in the camps' designs. This was often dictated by the availability of materials, the nature of the terrain, and other factors. The lack of a standard design also made planning each attack a new challenge to the enemy. There was no textbook solution; each plan of attack had to take into account the design and circumstances unique to each camp. The degree of imagination apparent in their design and defenses clearly demonstrated the initiative and practicality of Special Forces.

Design of the camps was constantly refined as a result of lessons learned and existing camps were upgraded. Given the many designs that were tried, it is unusual that a camp in the shape of a six-pointed star was never built, for such a design would have provided more interior space than the five-pointed star or triangle. An attacker would have had two choices for points of attack: either the strongly fortified point, which would receive supporting fire from its neighboring points; or into a re-entrant between two points, which they had to fight past and then take fire from both flanks from the arms of the star. The inner perimeter might be a hexagon with a corner bunker covering each arm.

In the final days of US involvement in the war, B-52 bombers cratered some of the camps abandoned by the ARVN. The new regime recovered concertina wire and other materials from some camps and used them elsewhere. Local inhabitants stripped the abandoned camps of useable materials.

Little remains of the camps today, those in the most remote locations having been abandoned and reclaimed by the jungle. As time has passed,

Overrun Camps

Camp	Date	CTZ	A-Team
Hiep Hoa	24 Nov 63	IV	A-21
Polei Krong	4 Jul 64	II	A-122
Dong Xoai	9 Jun 65	III	A-342
Dak Sut	18 Aug 65	II	A-218
A Shau	11 Mar 66	I	A-102
Lang Vei	7 Feb 68	I	A-101
Kham Duc*	10 May 68	I	A-105

* Evacuated while under attack.

bunkers have collapsed and berms and trenches have eroded away. In a few instances, villages grew out of abandoned camps, the local inhabitants moving into the stouter structures and conventional huts built around them. Others were bulldozed over to make way for cultivation or simply to erase any reminders of the war.

Special Forces still operates camps in remote lands, Honduras and Colombia for example, and they are not unlike their Vietnam predecessors.

Glossary

A-team	Special Forces operational detachment A
ARVN	Army of the Republic of Vietnam
CIDG	Civilian Irregular Defense Group (pronounced "sidge")
CMP	Corrugated Metal Pipe
CONEX	CONtainer EXpress shipping box
CRP	Combat Reconnaissance Platoon
CSF	Camp Strike Force
CTZ	Corps Tactical Zone
DEFCON	DEFensive CONcentration
LAW	Light Anti-armor Weapon
LLDB	Luc-luong Dac-Biét (Vietnamese Airborne Special Forces)
MIKE Force	Mobile strIKE Force
NVA	North Vietnamese Army
PSP	Pierced Steel Plank
RPG	Rocket Propelled Grenade
Seabees	Naval Construction Battalion (from the abbreviation "CB")
SFGA	Special Forces Group (Airborne)
TAOR	Tactical Area Of Responsibility
TOC	Tactical Operations Center
USSF	United States Special Forces
VC	Viet Cong

Bibliography

Donlon, Roger H., *Beyond Nam Dong*, Leavenworth, KS: R&N Publishers, 1998 (expanded edition of *Outpost of Freedom*, New York: McGraw-Hill, 1965)

Fall, Bernard B., *Street Without Joy*, Mechanicsburg, PA: Stackpole Books, 1964

Kelly, Francis J., *US Army Special Forces, 1961–1971* (Vietnam Studies series), Washington, DC: Department of the Army, 1973

Phillips, William J., *Night of the Silver Stars: The Battle of Lang Vei*, Annapolis, MD: Naval Institute Press, 1997

Simpson, Charles M., *Inside the Green Berets*, Novato, CA: Presidio Press, 1983

Stanton, Shelby, *Green Berets at War: US Army Special Forces in Southeast Asia 1956–1975*, Novato, CA: Presidio Press, 1985

Stanton, Shelby, *Special Forces at War: An Illustrated History, Southeast Asia 1957–1975*, Charlottesville, VA: Howell Press, 1990

Stockwell, David B., *Tanks in the Wire: The First Use of Enemy Armor in Vietnam*, Canton, OH: Daring Books, 1989

5th SFGA, *The Green Beret Magazine* Vol. I–V (5th SFGA monthly publication, 1966–70). Complete reprint set available from RADIX Associates, 2314 Cheshire Ln., Houston, TX 77018–4023, USA

Field Fortifications, FM 5-15, August 17, 1968. Copies of this and other field manuals may be purchased from Military/Info Publishing: http://www.military-info.com/Index.htm

Index